Love Emerges
when the
Mind Dissolves

**Other English-Language Books
by Yogmata Keiko Aikawa**

108 Teachings: The Path to the True Self
(Natus Books, 2020)

Empty Your Mind and Achieve Your Dreams
(Natus Books, 2020)

*The Road to Enlightenment: Finding the Way Through
Yoga Teachings and Meditation*
(Kodansha USA, 2014)

Love Emerges
when the
Mind Dissolves

Yogmata Keiko Aikawa

HIMALAYAN WISDOM SERIES

Natus Books
Barrytown, NY

Published by Natus Books
120 Station Hill Road
Barrytown, NY 12507

Natus Books is a publishing project of the Institute for
Publishing Arts, a not-for-profit, tax-exempt organization
[501(c)(3)].

Cover and interior design by Susan Quasha

ISBN: 978-158177-189-3

Library of Congress Control Number: 2019942353

Manufactured in the United States of America

Contents

CHAPTER FOUR

Aim for a True Way of Living

Love Emerges

when the

Mind Dissolves

Introduction

In pursuit of a peaceful soul

A big earthquake hit eastern Japan in 2011, and the pain that resulted from the calamity, in addition to the resulting disaster at the Fukushima nuclear power plant, was incalculable. Many people lost their families. Many homes were destroyed in the blink of an eye, washed away by the tsunami and swallowed into the sea. Nothing could be done in the face of the overwhelming power of nature. I offer my most sincere prayers for the souls of those who perished in the disaster. May those who were victims of the disaster be protected by God. I wish for their souls to be comforted and for their families to live through this difficulty with courage. In addition, I pray that people take this opportunity to think about true happiness and consider such disasters as a valuable lesson in life.

"What is our purpose here on earth?"

"How should I live the rest of my life?"

"Why is life sometimes so painful?"

"What can I do to be happy?"

No doubt we have all, at times, asked ourselves such questions.

Life offers many ways of coping with various feelings, and all of our lives are shaped by fate. Some of us may be stimulated by the discovery of something new while others are feeling bored and listless; some of us may be agonizing over work and/or human relationships while others are battling illness. Most of us continue to seek something in order to find happiness and grow as human beings, even if we encounter many obstacles.

We also work in order to live, and we look for rewards in life and work by putting our hearts and souls into both. We go on trips or go out to enliven our usual routines.

Although we may question ourselves every now and then, or occasionally fret over our way of life, we manage to live by meeting our basic needs for food, clothes, and shelter, and we feel generally satisfied that our lives are pretty good.

Nevertheless, problems and challenges occur from time to time, forcing us to confront such feelings as anger, anxiety, bitterness, doubt, jealousy, sadness, etc. This is exactly what the Japanese people are going through as they face the aftermath of the earthquake, tsunami, and ensuing nuclear accident, and these fears are not limited to those who were directly hit by these disasters. Such events sap people's vital energy, making their cells contract. Blood may not flow as readily, blood vessels harden, the nerves wear out, and these conditions manifest in the form of various diseases. Furthermore, exposure to misfortune on such a scale tends to harden people's spirits and change them into hard-hearted people.

Where does suffering come from?

Our experiences depend on many things, including environmental changes and the opportunities fate puts our way. Situations occur where we feel pain and agonize over our encounters, and we feel the agony must come from outside. We think obstacles enter from outside because we are unable to see them within ourselves; however, it actually is our inner minds that draw them in. We agonize over these obstacles because we have let them in. To put it simply, we are creating suffering for ourselves by reacting to our physical senses and obsessive memories of long ago, with various experiences and thoughts acting as catalysts.

How does the mind work, after all? When we look at the mind closely, we see an ocean of rippling waves filled with desire and suffering. But, deep within our minds and bodies, there is boundless stillness and love like the deepest waters. All things are born from this stillness. In it, there is an abundance of vital energy and mysterious force. This force can generate profound awareness in people and begin to dissolve suffering, so that we can be transformed into beings that are genuine and joyous. And what's more, this transformation is nonreversible—that is, we can be transformed and transcend our minds and bodies.

No easy task, you may be saying to yourself. Under normal circumstances, you would be right, but it becomes possible by putting something into practice, something I will explain and introduce you to in this book: grace from the Himalayas, in the form of the secret Himalayan Siddha teachings.

Generally speaking, the transformation and transcendence of consciousness is usually considered impossible. It is a process of cleansing the mind and body at the most profound level, maintaining balance, promoting awareness, being guided to a boundless stillness, and fostering growth. It is a path toward the ultimate consciousness, called true samadhi, where true success and enlightenment are brought on. However, it is not a path that anyone can access simply by choosing to.

I went to the Himalayas and I realized the true purpose of life as I was greeted by the grace of Himalaya. The profound love that emanates from the Himalayas has benefits—namely, its blessings sprinkle down on every corner of the world, transcending all boundaries. It is a boundless love that envelops everything, like the sun, and fills all it touches with warmth and light. Through trust, you too can be enveloped in this boundless light and be able to grow, full of vital energy. The light becomes sacred energy, invigorating all the cells in your body and strengthening your vital force at the source as it enfolds you in joy.

That's right. There is the sun at your source. Please be sure to notice this sun. Your inner sun is your vital force, from which you are able to draw out further mysterious forces from within. The sun shining in the giant sky and the sun hidden within are both teaching us the wonder of giving and the wonder of shining by letting go. The sun gives life to all beings; it continues to patiently offer blessings. It simply shines, fills, and continues to give.

Why can't we exist like the sun? Why can't we transform into beings that continue to patiently give, expecting nothing in return? Are we not able to use our energy in this way?

Remove impurities and clouds

People live their lives by exhausting their minds on too many matters. At times they are aware of this; at other times they are completely unaware. The problem is that the mind doesn't know how to rest; this uses up energy and causes people to burn out. For example, when people get sick, they long to be healthy. Once they get well and become healthy again, they begin to expect other things. Similarly, there is no end to people's desires as they continue to want to improve their relationships with people, want their work to be satisfying, their company to grow, their love life to be fulfilling, their family to be happy, to acquire knowledge, to be challenged by new experiences, etc. These desires come along one after another and are endless.

Still, people are able to live with desires while keeping their minds active. They rejoice with a sense of fulfilment once their desires are realized, but this fulfilment is merely one small part of that person's senses, feelings, and mind. That joy, the object of their joy and feelings of satisfaction, will disappear one day. Indeed, the joy can turn into anxiety and fear, the more you desire to have it last forever. If you are under stress, there is always anxiety lurking, even when you feel happy. The mind always works like this. What's needed, then, is a certain profound awareness—an awareness of the truth.

For example, people worry about their children. When their children have grown up, they feel lonely, even though they know their children are supposed to leave the nest and build their own homes. I have known instances where, when families have stayed together, family members have felt tied down to each other, and have ended up hurting each other and getting distressed. There is always joy and pain in the parent/child relationship, which is perpetually shifting. The same can be said about husband and wife: the relationship becomes trying if there is too much dependence on each other; each must show an understanding of the other.

It is crucial to focus on the mind at its source by cleansing and releasing it as you realize its prejudiced views. By connecting to the truth at the core of your own consciousness, to the genuine love from genuine mind and to peace and the ultimate life force, you will be able to see more clearly and better able to respond to the changes around you, while feeling more at peace within yourself. It is important to learn this new way of living by putting it into actual practice.

As I mentioned earlier, there is boundless love and the stillness of deep waters within us; these can heal you by turning into a profound peace of mind. However, people have many desires and experiences through which many thoughts surge, attaching impurities to their minds. This causes the mind to be agitated, and the serene deep waters that are contained within it cannot be seen, having been blurred by the agitated waves above. People's minds in this state can be likened to a pure blue sky obscured by clouds.

The things that adhere to the insides of people's minds include obsessions, memories, knowledge, and feelings. These can all be classified as traumas. They have made their way into people's psyches, causing them to react, compare, think, doubt, and judge. Unless you can see the calm waters beneath, there is no serenity. Without it, people are unable to heal or rest.

In order to access the calm, deep waters, it is essential to remove the splashing waves and impurities by cleansing. Unfortunately, they are not easily removed because they are ingrained in the soul as fate and karma. However, we can expedite the return to our true, pure selves by putting into practice the secret teachings of the Himalayan Siddha masters. But please be advised: while there are many moral teachings and/or lessons of the mind available, not to mention doctrines of an inner psychological world which usually involve encounters with various teachers, these tend to create new, equally unhelpful obsessions in the mind. True freedom and liberation of the mind can only be acquired through the true samadhi. Through the wisdom of the bioscience-based teachings of the Himalayan Siddha masters, you can be safely and expeditiously guided to existence at its true source.

A small revelation called "awareness"

In removing clouds, one of the most valuable teachings is "to become aware." No matter how much you are told about what's correct and good by others, or how much you read books on morality, etc., unless there is your own awakening and awareness, nothing can be gained, and no true sense of liberation will come your way. Everything starts by becoming aware; it is the key to getting closer to the truth as you let go of clouds and impurities of the mind. But what should you do to enhance awareness? To this to happen, you must first begin to accept yourself as you are. Then you can begin to remove and cleanse clouds and traumas within you, one by one, and learn how to love yourself. The way to do this is through meditation.

Through the various workshops, prayers, and meditation techniques of the Anugraha Himalayan Samadhi Program you can begin to move toward your true self as you untangle and release one by one what the mind,

Encounter the truth by feeling the stillness, grandeur, and profound love of the Himalyas body, and consciousness are all about. Additionally, you will begin to realize what your true self and true happiness is and begin to walk toward your goal while feeling safe and secure. That's right—awareness can manifest gradually through small revelations. These can happen in various stages of meditation, from surface level to deep level, or they can happen in your everyday life. At times, it's perfectly acceptable for these small revelations to be something quite mundane.

For example, when you wake up in the morning and hesitate over what to wear that day, you will notice, "Ah, this is one of my unhelpful obsessions." Then, gradually, your intuition kicks in and you won't hesitate next time. As you experience these small revelations one after the other daily, one day you will be transported into the realm of deep meditation where you have followed through various meditative stages of the secret Himalayan Siddha teachings. Then you will be able to encounter your true self, where the source of everything is brought forth in the stillness we associate with deep waters. Once you have encountered your true self you will be able to live by swimming through your life with ease, no matter how rough the seas become. Don't you think it would be a shame to reach the end of your life without experiencing this?

Thanks to the secret Himalayan Siddha teachings, your inner self can be awakened through Anugraha (power as wellspring of creativity) and by receiving diksha (energy initiation). Once you are blessed with this diksha, you are awarded with a high level of energy initiation, and based on this, your body and mind are awakened and purified. As you continue to receive diksha, you will be safely and expeditiously transformed. In addition, once you proceed with various types of meditative training involving sound or light to promote cleansing, a deep state of meditation occurs, and you will be able to encounter your true self. This can occur through workshops, prayers, or meditations while receiving the blessings of Anugraha. In this way, as you deepen awareness and through the process of unraveling, your mind will gradually be released, and you will be able to live your life effortlessly.

To purify everything within ourselves, to cleanse our bodies and minds and turn into our true selves, means to become the sun. And this is our true purpose in life.

YOGMATA KEIKO AIKAWA

CHAPTER ONE

Why do we meditate?

1. Your Wishes Can Be Fulfilled

Conflicts occur due to needy mind

Why do so many of us feel so impoverished when our society is inundated with material goods? Why does peace so rarely follow relentless conflict? People's minds are always obsessing over something and for this reason they are always burdened with all kinds of difficulties.

What are the issues that you feel burdened by? Perhaps you are concerned about the future, or perhaps you are experiencing problems at work, with your workmates or your employer. Or perhaps things aren't good at home, or your health isn't what you would like it to be. Perhaps you are concerned about ecological or social issues, or you fret about politics and the economy. When you remove yourself from your immediate context and look at the world, you see chaos and war—chaos caused by differences in politics and economics, global environmental issues, the destruction of nature, natural disasters like the recent earthquakes, problems with nuclear power, etc.

While certain societies continue to prosper and grow, problems continue to pile up in a vortex of confusion, insecurity, hatred, and anger. The world is continually being recast in the image of hatred due to differences in belief, ethnicity, economy, the gap between the haves and the have-nots, etc. Behind a superficially friendly mood there exists rivalry, jealousy, and hatred; the seeds of conflict are lurking in many corners of the world. In short, we have become narrow-minded. There is no place left where love can exist. We are no longer able to receive love, let alone give it. Wisdom disappears also: we have given up searching for our own truth and are content merely to believe what others say.

The inner peaceful existence is forgotten

My own journey in search of the truth took me a long time and led me ultimately to the Himalayas. Since then I have visited the Himalayas many times and met with many Siddha masters. They are truly pure, natural, and free human beings, equipped with wonderful powers. From these masters I was able to receive the most wonderful gift—inner peace. Unfortunately, most of us deplete our inner reserves by exhausting the mind in wasteful ways. Forgetting our inner tranquility and inner self, we allow our mind to drive us on without purpose or aim.

When people's senses are stimulated by something, it is communicated to the mind. Once the mind begins to function, the potentially interminable process of identification and selection begins. When identification begins to operate, it leads in turn to comparison and judgment, and the mind becomes dazzled and obsessed with good or bad, like or dislike, win or lose, in the process. And the mind works by reacting and taking action—by discovering differences in others, fearing them, attacking for self-defense, pulling back, feeling safe, etc. When the mind operates in this way, complicated thoughts get tangled through comparison and doubt, rather than winnowed out through trust. We often work ourselves up even more by avoiding things that need our attention or by numbing our minds when we feel tense, so that we become even more confused and can never rest, even when we want to.

The reactive mind has accumulated impressions and obsessions from various experiences from the past, and thoughts and feelings tend to evolve one after the other as you react to them through stimulation. It doesn't matter whether these things are positive or negative; thoughts themselves associate and evolve on their own. When this becomes excessive, you can't get rid of feeling tired, no matter how many hours you sleep. And if you don't get enough sleep, you will eventually suffer from insomnia. Depending on who you are, this may lead to overeating or attempts to somehow restore mental balance, perhaps by taking a break or seeking some sort of change. We live our lives by doing our best, bumping along, sometimes anxious and sometimes enjoying ourselves, feeling alternately lost and proud; we resign ourselves to the fact that this is life, after all. However, this is not truly a life of wisdom.

Samadhi means "zanmai" (a perfect spiritual concentration)

What, then, is a life of true wisdom like? The secret teachings of the Himalayan Siddha masters will guide you to this way of life; then, the godlike wisdom you inherently possess will begin to manifest. You can only access the richness within by practicing meditation. Through meditation, you will be able to acquire spiritual tranquility, becoming your true self. This takes place in back of where the eye can see and beyond the tangible, at the source of existence where love, peace, and wisdom are abundant.

The path to the true self is usually closed, but you can step onto it, thanks to the secret teachings of the Himalayan Siddha masters. The various sacred training techniques start with meditation and prayer, and, under normal conditions, are closely guarded. I was very fortunate to have been taught them and, as a result, to have found the truth, by attaining ultimate samadhi. It is my aim, in this book, to share these teachings about the truth with those who are seeking it.

When you are engrossed in something, concentrating on one single area of interest, it is difficult for anything else to enter your mind. Your eyes are reluctant to see; your ears are reluctant to hear. It is almost as if you have transcended space and time to become one with the object of your interest. Similarly, there are various levels at which samadhi can be targeted, and to be pursuing something in a specialized field is not an altogether different process: in order to evolve the self, one aims for the very best object. You can encounter the highest samadhi by experiencing deep meditation, and you will be taught how to do so in the pages of this book.

Change yourself through meditation and change those around you

Wisdom can be defined as the ability to judge matters correctly. A strong will is useful here and we will speak in this book of a genuine willpower called *sankalpah*. When the mind is not certain, has no confidence, and is pulled in a negative direction, it cannot be pure since the willpower weakens and intentions cannot progress. For sankalpah, a pure mind is needed, and in order to acquire sankalpah, you need to cleanse your mind and cultivate your trust. Your mind will be purged, and your confidence will increase as you pass through the stages of meditative practice.

What do you think meditation is? It is often regarded a means to relax the mind and body, as a kind of vague, sleep-induced state. However, this is not real meditation; real meditation awakens you rather than making you drowsy. Your inner self is gradually awakened and purified, and your awareness and understanding increase. The secret teachings of the Himalayan Siddha masters include various meditation techniques. One of them is Siddha kriya meditation. A *Siddha* is an accomplished

Who on Earth am I?

master who has attained the ultimate samadhi, and this meditation technique enables us to manage life's energy, called *kriya*. A vital energy called *prana* purifies life's energy along paths in the body called *nadi*. In addition, one of the life energies, fire energy (generated by kriya technique), burns accumulated stress and attachments in the body and mind, bringing us into a deep meditative state.

Another meditation technique, focused on sound, is known as samadhi meditation. In this meditation, you are first led in a prayer meditation to increase purification and trust, followed by an initiation ceremony of *Anugraha* (the grace of existence at its true source). After this, you will be initiated into a meditative state using sound. This sound is a sacred sound called a *mantra*; it is given to you by a Siddha master and is very different from anything that can be learned from a book—it has a live power. As you continue to proceed with this training, you will start to receive *diksha* of a higher order. Through these auditory waves, while chanting the mantra, you will eventually acquire enlightenment. The mantra's waves—which are purity in themselves—control energy within and reach all the way to the true source of life.

There are various other meditation techniques, such as chakra meditation, creative meditation, and awareness meditation. The techniques that best suit you will be revealed to you as required.

Purify energy of the ego

In life, we are continually exposed to other people's thoughts, opinions, and ideas. Sometimes they are better than ours, and our minds need to be flexible if we are to lend an ear to them. Our egos often enter the fray, to protect ourselves out of competitive spirit. Ego can also be defined as desire. The stronger our ego and the deeper our desire, the more likely it is that our self-assertion will develop into a dispute. This is different from an assertion expressed for the benefit of truth or an assertion made on behalf of the happiness of others. In such cases, we must remember that we are not only competing against the other person but also fighting with ourselves—indeed, the fact that we are at odds with others actually means that we are also in conflict with ourselves. Becoming too engrossed in this mode can only lead to pain.

Suffering makes people obstinate; it binds them down, poisons their bodies, and induces stress. This suffering must somehow be released. Those who give up on their suffering and those who remain unaware of it continue to be burdened by it, often blaming others for their suffering, simply through ignorance. Often, the only thing that changes things is death, but death is of the physical body only—our suffering continues to be stored on the astral plane. The important thing to understand is that, because we have bodies, we may cleanse ourselves of the attachments and ego energy that make it harder for us to live fulfilling lives. Meditation can release us not only from current suffering, but also from the suffering after death and the suffering of being reborn. Furthermore, it can even purify ancestors to whom we are linked.

No matter the era, there have always been wars—wars that cause pain, both to individuals and to nations. When traced to the source, these wars are all triggered by disputes between the minds of people. There may be those who consider war a necessary evil, provided it paves the way for peace; there is tremendous risk involved, however, when you can only learn and advance by risking death. Peace is always more welcome if it can be achieved without fighting a war. There would be a greater likelihood of this happening if we could persuade more people to become awakened and enlightened through meditation. We can all meditate in the direction of love and peace by moving away from egotistical assertions. By having all the peoples of the world practice meditation, peace in the world would certainly become a more attainable reality. Those who remain unaware of the deep love that surpasses the ego will bear the burden of their suffering until they die; however, as I mentioned earlier, this suffering knows no end, even after death.

By meditating, with the guidance of the secret teachings of the Himalayan Siddha masters, you can become a person of wisdom who is able to establish peace and love within. Further, you will bear the responsibility of conveying this true way of living, by passing on what you have learned to those around you, through your meditation practice and by describing your transformational experiences. I would very much like you to share the wisdom and love you have acquired with those who are lost, those who don't know what to do because they are unable to see beyond, and those who feel anxious because they can't see what lies ahead, no matter how hard they try. This is the way to change the world.

Awareness through meditation

Meditation is a process in which you feel the flow of becoming one with the power of peace and love that fills from within, by purifying the body and mind through various techniques. There are many levels of energy within us; we are made up of various energies that fuse together. Through meditation, these energies converge as one—that is, a state of oneness is created.

The act of meditation displays nothing to those who view it from the outside. But, within, you are cleansing yourself of all your confused energies, bringing your overall energy to an altogether higher level by bringing your various energies together as one and filling them with vital energy to create a state of deep relaxation. Through this process, you will begin to realize what you have been so caught up in and what you have been dwelling on. Your mind will loosen, and you will be able to see its condition clearly; you will come to know its workings and allow it to be emptied. By realizing how mundane the matters you dwelled on were, the preoccupations that you have tied to yourself will begin to peel away from you one by one. As this happens, you can let go the self. Along with increased awareness, your mind will become empty and purified, and any distortions to the body will be modified, leaving you feeling refreshed, recharged, and revived.

We don't usually see how our mind works internally; unless we awaken our consciousness, we are not in the right state to become aware of it. In addition, under a busy schedule of rushing to and from work, our energy is trapped in a disrupted condition, just as we are trapped by our desires and obsessions—in a state of total chaos. Because of this, we don't notice our inner selves and we live our lives holding simultaneously conflicting views and feeling stressed. To live in such a way is to live at the mercy of karma, and to continue in this way is to run the risk of becoming closed-minded and negative, or worse—sick, exhausted, and burned out. No matter how much you take pride in being tough, an exhausted mind can't be healed that easily; your mental fatigue will eventually catch up with you and manifest as some type of distortion. The secret teachings of the Himalayan Siddha masters open the path to true health and spiritual enlightenment, releasing people from their distorted states and guiding them to true happiness.

Meditation is rebirth and casting-off of dead skin

Meditation is a process of being born again—"a practice to surpass death." It is a profound stillness of creative existence at its source. And people are born from this stillness. It is a beginning and a continuation of living, of being active, making the mind work, and accumulating karma, and it ends in stillness, with death. Although people cannot experience the beginning of the universe from creative existence at its source, they can acknowledge the end by experiencing death. The end and the beginning are the same—the end *is* the beginning. You will come to know this truth. Once you enter stillness, you will experience true self and God; this signifies rebirth, where body and mind perish and reincarnate. This is true samadhi, which can also be described as nirvana: a means of purifying the body and mind, deepening understanding, transforming old into new, understanding the connections between all of these things, working to link them through love, then entering into stillness and transcending them all.

Just as a room gets dusty after it has been lived in for a while, so our insides become filled with "dust" over time. We clean and dust when rooms get dirty, right? In the same way, we can reinvigorate ourselves by cleaning our bodies and minds from time to time, to restore balance. In doing so, life's energy can be revived. When I explain these concepts at lectures, there are occasionally people who misunderstand me and ask, "How can meditation revive life's force when all you are doing is sitting quietly?" Or, "Isn't it actually the reverse—doesn't meditation weaken you instead?" However, the secret teachings of the Himalayan Siddha masters are based on a profound meditation practice in which something inside us is powerfully transformed. There is nothing else like this, which both strengthens existence at a very high order while also reinforcing and reinvigorating the vital energies.

By continuing to diligently meditate, you will come to know your true essence as you feel the vital energy that resides deep within, and you will begin to feel confident. When that confidence deepens, you will no longer feel anxious or be frightened of death. While you can reap substantial rewards in quite a short time by meditating, it is crucial to continue to do so for your entire life. Once you are rested through meditation, even meditating for a short time will afford you profound rest and allow you to revive your power. It is truly a tonic for the soul. Sometimes, when we take long naps, we don't wake up feeling refreshed; on the contrary, it often happens that we feel even more tired. This is because fatigue caused by a confused state of mind and conflicted energies can't be solved through sleep alone. The core of fatigue can only be removed through meditation. Once you begin to be able to acquire profound rest through meditation, you will no longer need so many hours of sleep. This is because you will no longer be wasting energy through inner confusion or unnecessary attachments.

Assume the state of mindlessness: empty the mind

Become a peaceful, enriched person through meditation

As your inner self undergoes significant changes through meditation, you will become a person of joy, your thoughts turning positive and creative in every area of your life. You will become motivated and productive at home and at work, happily accepted in society, and successful in all your endeavors. Moreover, through meditation, once you encounter your true self, you can rid yourself of pain by seeking peace within yourself. The important thing is to regularly put meditation into practice, to make it part of your everyday life and to continue practicing it.

The Japanese people have always struck me as remarkably competent, and I am particularly reminded of this when I return from overseas. When I come back from a trip abroad, as soon as I land at the airport, I am struck once again by the subtle sensitivity of the Japanese people—their fastidiousness and care. Each country, of course, has its own unique style and character, formed in large part by its environment. The very religious Indian people, for example, appear to live each day in a somewhat carefree and accepting manner; they consider everything to be due to God's blessings and accept their circumstances in life. At the same time, however, they are world leaders in the field of computer science. Are science and spirituality polar opposites really? The Indian people seem able to bring their faith and resilience to bear on both.

It is common to see people begging on the street in India; for the Japanese, such behavior is completely out of question. They fear hunger and abhor poverty, and continually work to improve the quality of their lives. I liken this to riding a unicycle endlessly: you are not allowed to relax even for an instant and can do nothing but continue to pedal forever. There is a surprising number of people who feel that this type of living suits them just fine. They appear to be able to maintain their balance of mind by pedaling along in this way—doing so makes them feel they are progressing, and the sense of forward movement makes them feel secure.

Become someone who can control oneself

However, even if we think we are suited to this type of pedaling, fatigue will eventually set in, without fail. The time will come time when we will need to take pause. And then, even if we want to rest, we have no idea what to do to get rid of our fatigue, or how to change pace for a diversion. For this reason, we give ourselves up to pleasure too much—we eat and drink too much, feeling that, by doing so, we are somehow refreshing ourselves, setting ourselves up to embark in a new direction. But this is not real rest or serenity, and one day, we will find our energies further eroded, as our minds and bodies continue to wear down.

Sometimes people engage in hobbies and sports to such an all-consuming extent that they lose their spirit of adventure and inquisitive mind. Others simply give up, having been worn down by human relations or burned out by overly competitive work. Some people seek to escape stress by going on a journey or quest to find themselves. Others attend self-enlightenment seminars which only cause their minds to become further confused. Some people seek what they are looking for in nature or by retreating from society, as if the natural world can compensate for what they lack within. What they need, however, is nature from within.

There are those, again, whose mindset is so resoundingly negative that they know no peace of mind. They blame themselves, their parents, society, or the environment for not being able to accept things as they are. They become overly critical and seclude themselves in their rooms as they become increasingly depressed. They are not aware of how they feel inside at all and have no idea how to get out of their situation. What, then, can we do, if we are to live lives filled with wisdom, free and full of life's energy? To rescue people from difficulty is to suspend all action. By becoming aware, on your own, you can transform so that you are able to control yourself. Meditation will allow you to access the peace of mind that your present confusion has rendered invisible. Through meditation, you can awaken your mind, rest it at the same time, fine-tune it, and restore its luster.

Let's all wake up to this new way of living and meet our true selves. The inner journey of meditation will enable you to trace back to your beginning, and, by doing so, deepen understanding, release yourself from confusion, and live the life you desire with love and peace. Let's access the means of transforming into our best possible selves and living our best possible lives.

2. Meditation leads to success

What you gain by doing away with everything

I have been involved with yoga, meditation, and natural foods since I was in my teens. I eventually began to operate a yoga class and became an advocate for yoga in Japan. Good fortune was visited upon me in 1984. I will go into detail in Chapter 3, but, in brief, through a television project, one of the most famous Himalayan masters, Pilot Babaji, visited Japan to conduct an underground samadhi. I assisted in the project, and when everything was finished, Babaji approached me and asked me, "Why don't you come to Himalaya and train there?"

Here I must briefly explain what an underground samadhi is. An underground samadhi involves staying alone for many days, purifying the mind and body in an underground cave—so that everything from the outside world is shut out—and becoming one with the divine by transcending death. You may have heard of hatha yoga, which involves slowing down one's breathing and entering a state akin to hibernation, after which, the body must be massaged back to its original state. In an underground samadhi, the ultimate state is sought via awakening and transcendence. This ultimate samadhi is nirvana—nature's purest and utmost consciousness and bliss, proof of true enlightenment in which the body and mind are cleansed, the sensory organs controlled, death transcended, and a person becomes light by going beyond time and space, surpassing everything and ultimately becoming Brahman—that is, at one with the universe and completely in the present.

In India, samadhi is considered the best world that a human can possibly seek, and those who attain it are respected as Siddha masters. There are masters who immerse themselves in samadhi in the deepest and remotest parts of the Himalayas. However, it is important to stress that the underground samadhi is a highly advanced type of practice; quite a few people have lost their lives by attempting to practice it.

It is said that, in India, there are as many as twenty million ascetics who have renounced the world. It has also been said that someone attains samadhi underground once every several hundred years. Underground samadhi has become an aspiring practice among ascetics, and it is now said that samadhi is attained underground once every few decades.

The cave where the underground samadhi takes place is completely closed from above; unless someone opens the "lid," you will die. When I began to train in the Himalayas, hoping to become the first woman ever to succeed at this tremendously risky ascetic practice, I was desperate to know more and would recklessly throw myself into as many different types of spiritual pursuit as I could. One day, the master said to me, "Renounce everything." I was devastated. As I pondered what renouncing everything would mean, I felt scared and afraid. I wasn't able to realize, then, that so much could be gained by forsaking everything. I am not suggesting that you need to renounce everything; the crucial thing is not to overuse your mind, even to the point of stopping if from working. To stop the mind from working means to free yourself from obstructive thoughts—that is, to empty the mind. In this way, you will be able to rid yourself of all kinds of unnecessary attachments and obsessions.

You can build better human relationships through your own growth

When you dig deep down and examine your inner self, you will identify moments when you didn't behave as well as you might have done and realize that, through hurting other people's feelings, you also hurt yourself. It was simply your ego getting in the way. In a competitive society such as our own, you must win over others, or you end up losing. If you win over others, you can brag about your success.

If you feel you are more capable than others, you feel satisfied; if you feel inferior or make mistakes, you lose confidence and feel depressed. And so your mind goes up and down like a yo-yo and is never at rest. The fabric of society is comprised of interpersonal exchanges; we all encounter many people and forge numerous relationships in daily life. However, how many of these relationships can we say are good relationships? How many of the people we know can we really trust and depend on? It is up to us whether we build good interpersonal relationships or not, and we can forge better relationships by making ourselves grow as people. For this to happen, we must become aware—aware that, in the past, we have acted out of ignorance, been too quick to find fault with others, and hurt others through our actions. Perhaps you feel no need to do this; perhaps you are of an affable disposition and able to make your way through life without difficulty. However, even if this is the case, you may still be unsure of your true purpose in life and may not feel the deep satisfaction that comes from within.

One day, the master said to me, "Renounce everything"

If you are distressed, those around you are too

We often restrict ourselves and our actions. We tell ourselves that we ought to be kind to people, eat the right kinds of food, get enough sleep, etc. But we are strange creatures and our natures are such that, when we restrict ourselves in this way, we itch to do something that goes directly against the guidelines we have imposed on ourselves—we are inadvertently mean when we intend to be nice, etc. Why? By simply deciding what you ought to do and how you ought to behave, you create a certain level of obsession within. When that obsession becomes too strong, what you have taken for granted acquires an unnatural force. Luckily, the secret teachings of the Himalayan Siddha masters can free your mind of its obsessions and prejudices, which will peel away quite naturally as your awareness increases. Through this type of meditation, you can evolve your consciousness and become enlightened through the wisdom and message of Buddha. You don't need to think about anything as you meditate and your mind starts to melt, allowing you to access your core with a clear and open heart.

You don't need to push yourself. There is no need to force yourself to become a good person or to overexert yourself in any way. Simply do nothing while establishing inner peace and love. I am not in a position to dictate anything in terms of how you should conduct yourself at work. I am no expert where professions are concerned, and neither do I assume the role of teaching you "how to succeed." However, there is one thing that I can convey to you with conviction: the universe is within yourself. It is my belief—and my experience—that you can know everything by purifying your inner self, awakening, and becoming peaceful. This in turn leads to the profound insight and intuition that are often so necessary for success.

Meditation will change your surroundings

When you meditate and as your mind becomes transparent, a pure will—or purpose, or determination—kicks in. This is called *sankalpah*. By cleansing your body and mind with confidence and faith, you can get closer to the supreme existence and receive its blessings. In order for this to happen, you must trust completely in your meditation practice. As you become more aware, your mind will rid itself progressively of received notions, your thoughts will become true, and you will be able to use sankalpah more effectively, which, in turn, will help you to maximize your life's potential. When you can stay happy, positive, and serene for all twenty-four hours of the day, you will know that the sacred waves are within you. Then, simply by being close to you, those around you will feel purified and become filled with happiness. This demonstrates the extent to which our inner state can influence others, which is because we are all linked in a profound way. If we are enjoying ourselves, those around us feel happy; if we suffer, those around us feel distressed too.

Your words and actions, your philosophy and lifestyle, affect those around you. However, it is a challenge to try to change those around you, and, in fact, rather than *trying* to change them, we should *allow* them to change. Through living by example and demonstrating how to live with a peaceful and positive attitude, those around you will gradually feel more energetic. Naturally, work efficiency will improve, but family life will also benefit. Your inner transformation will change those around you. That is, your meditation practice changes your surroundings, and these ripples will be felt in your family and workplace, in society and in the world. It is in this sense that I mean, quite seriously, that your meditation practice can play a role in improving world peace.

When you change, those around you will change

Reset your own state of mind to zero

I am facing you, wishing you happiness, and, by not stopping there, I am wishing peace for the world. These waves from samadhi through me are a gift from God, and they reach you at an invisible, profound level. The transmission of this type of high-level waves is born from a state of samadhi called *shaktipat*. Shaktipat is a high-level energy initiation and blessing, which comes in various forms. It can be transmitted through diksha, transmitted with a touch, by a look, by foot, or with a sacred word. As you know, a Yogi (practitioner of Yoga) who has attained the ultimate samadhi is referred to as a Siddha, and a spiritual teacher is called a Siddha master. Siddha masters are transmitting shaktipat—in all its forms—to every one of you.

An energy induction that awakens you with the goal of transforming you into a spiritual person is referred to as Siddha diksha. Once you are bestowed with this, your mind is swiftly cleansed and will be ready to receive Anugraha energy at all times. Through this, you cleanse and heal at a deep level, banishing idle thoughts and deepening the level of your meditation. In order to awaken and acquire absolute happiness and enlightenment by cleansing, you need to undergo certain ascetic training. For this to happen, you need to be enlightened to take that journey, and introduced to the secret meditation technique appropriate for each level. That initiation begins with the appropriate stage of diksha. A Siddha master's samadhi power lies in the waves of Anugraha. When you meditate, these waves transmit and induce a feeling of happiness within you. With a meditation practice connected to Anugraha, you can act as a bridge, transmitting peaceful waves to those around you. If others do the same, followed by yet others again, waves will gradually transmit to all the peoples of the world, and we may see a day when peace in the world becomes a reality. I would go so far as to say that peace *will* become a reality, if all the peoples of the world practice meditation.

In order to deepen your meditation, acquire true happiness, and be truly enlightened, it is essential that you trust yourself as a profoundly pure self, believe in the existence of the profound creative source, and place confidence in your master as the right bridge for you. Your true self, the divinity, and the master are one and the same. The master is the door to success, true happiness, and enlightenment, and the blessings of the master flow from the eyes, hands, and feet. The question is: Are you ready to receive them, by surrendering and through trust?

In India, people usually welcome wandering saints with joy; the philosophy of love is well established. People believe that when an ascetic visits their home their family members are purified. They not only welcome saints, but trainee monks as well. This type of traditional practice and the warm welcome with which it is received is fully preserved to this day. As a result, the people of India are able to live in harmony even with the intermingling of different religious sects. India was originally a Hindu nation—God's religion for the masses. Then Buddhism was introduced, followed by Islam and Christianity, all of which are still in evidence there today. Buddhism was less prevalent in medieval times but has enjoyed a resurgence since World War II. In the past, Islamic kings converted many people to Islam, just as the nation was colonized by Christianity, but factionalism and discord have been overcome by peaceful, loving minds.

The secret teachings of the Himalayan Siddha masters are not based on doctrine as such; they are concerned with inner truth and God's truth. Practical meditation is taught and cannot be violated—it will always exist. Perhaps, as you are reading this, you are thinking to yourself that conflicts do occur in India from time to time, and that this fact surely contradicts what I am saying. I believe there are many reasons for this, one of which is that religious conflict elsewhere in the world is affecting the psyche of the Indian people, although I still think a deep yearning for peace remains. The Japanese people are very different, of course, but I think the very fact that so many different value systems and religious beliefs are intertwined is an excellent argument for being inducted into meditation practice, in which the individual's inner growth is promoted and it is possible to encounter the divine on an individual basis.

As India was in the past, I pray that each one of us will come to believe in creative existence and ourselves and encounter the path to becoming enlightened through the force of meditation. Creeds which involve learning through doctrine alone seek, essentially, to increase the mind's knowledge so that the body can die more successfully; such an approach can only lead to power struggles between those who hold different beliefs.

Bring on boundless creative power

Unfortunately, as we continue to make remarkable scientific progress, the older wisdoms seem to be on the wane. As a result, we live a life of convenience but have become so used to it that we are no longer equipped to tolerate or deal with the slightest inconvenience. We could almost say that this situation has become the new religion. Because of this, we are running the risk of losing something precious, which we might variously think of as trust, the gentle soul, or wisdom. Have our souls ever been as diminished as they are now? Even as new cures for diseases are discovered and our life spans are extended, our vital forces are waning because we have lost our spiritual richness and wisdom. This is because our creative power is generated from within—from our inner richness.

I am repeating myself, I know, but trust is crucial if you are to meditate successfully. As you begin to purge yourself of negative energy, you may experience surges of negative emotions from the past—anger, anxiety, doubt, sadness, etc. If this does happen, it is a necessary step in the process of transformation and rebirth. We have all been doubtful, angry, etc., at some point in our lives; these feelings are ours to claim as our own, and we should acknowledge them and take them to heart. Then, you release yourself from them and let them be flushed away. We are often quick to notice things about other people, but reluctant to acknowledge those same things in ourselves. To be awakened means to know what's inside. The pain that we find there is caused by the ego; to become aware of the ego requires work, and it may, depending on the kind of person you are, be a somewhat painful process.

The mind works without limits, powered by its self-defense mechanism. It is no easy task to stop the mind from working with a view to eventually emptying it—the mind has no "off" switch. However, the fact that you are aware will inevitably lead to releasing attachments, and then you are on your way to becoming free. This is called awareness meditation. Cleansing can be accelerated through kriya meditation, which uses fire energy invigorated by prana to burn away unnecessary attachments. The vital energy, prana, is what keeps us alive; it is generated from creative existence at its source. In addition to an awareness-enhancing meditation practice, the Anugraha Himalayan Samadhi Program includes many cleansing exercises for body and mind, all of which proactively help to bring about a swift rebirth.

Work performance significantly differs depending on whether you meditate or not

Modern society has become so convenient, so glutted with material goods, that our life force has diminished to such an extent that our bodies are merely nexuses of illness. We have become debilitated by dependence, and, because human relationships can be complicated in competitive society, we feel stressed in everything. Stress causes illness and disease, and wreaks havoc on our internal organs, causing cancer, mental disorders, etc. Our bodies and minds struggle to maintain their balance. The Himalayan masters believed in God and discovered how to control the body and mind, and how to maintain the two in balance in order to further purify them through the wisdom of samadhi. This is a path to the divine in the truest sense of the word, on which you will become your true self and acquire genuine happiness.

There is a physical pose, called *asana*, which helps to maintain balance. Through it, you can remove bodily distortions and reset your spine and pelvis. You can also practice ascetic exercises, sometimes involving sound and light, in order to strengthen your equilibrium by tapping into the subtle energies of the astral body. Remember, your body is the universe itself; you will know everything, transform, surpass, and become your authentic self by relinquishing and further exploring it. Perhaps, as you read this, you are worrying about how you will continue to live your life: How will you possibly get everything done if you are meditating all the time in an attempt to expand your awareness? However, I am not suggesting that you meditate from morning to night; I am merely suggesting that you set aside a little time each day, and that it is important to do so if you are intent on developing a meditation routine.

Just as we are all different, so are our ideas about what transforming ourselves might mean. Nevertheless, I firmly believe that we can *all* become happy as a result of burning off karma, cleansing ourselves, and living life with peace of mind. If you have goals in mind that you are keen to achieve, meditating diligently will only help. "Prove it," you may well ask, but it is never easy to prove the effects of meditation to those who have yet to experience them. It is, however, common for us to consider mysterious teachings, teachings that go far beyond words, as the only solution when confronted by serious illness, problems with family, etc.—situations that cannot be remedied by seeking the advice of traditional doctors or by spending money.

We all have different values and our priorities differ as to how we should spend our lives; most of us focus on pleasuring the senses and earning money. Those of us who are active in the business world prioritize work; but it is still important to evolve, and to practice self-care on the mind and body. My belief—as you have surely realized by now—is that the most effective way to do this, to fundamentally refresh and revive life's force, is to start at the very root of it all. To put meditation into practice is to balance and heal yourself through purification. And, by harnessing your true self at its source, you will receive the blessings of life's energy, become a person of wisdom, and become enlightened. This is the point at which you can live peacefully and successfully, making yourself happy as well as those around you.

3. Know How to Use Energy Through Meditation

A little dissatisfaction can become the seed of illness

One way to think of illness is to regard it as the body's way of balancing energy. We become ill when our immune system is weakened due to an imbalance caused by karma—perhaps our lifestyle is too disruptive, or our minds are overly burdened with unhealthy attachments. The mind, as we have mentioned, always tries to regain balance using its self-healing ability and natural recuperative power. Symptoms, then, are the external signs that our body is fighting illness. It is hard for us to realize, calmly, that there must have been a reason for the imbalance which caused the illness. What, then, should we do? We can at least proactively seek a better balance, and trust that we will be cured of whatever ails us.

Trust and gratitude are key components to maintaining balance—always try to privilege them over anxiety. Being positive helps us to think of illness as a positive thing, an opportunity to look at ourselves, to reflect and be grateful. Even a serious illness presents us with an opportunity to review and reflect on our lifestyle, to see what went wrong. We can then mend our ways by exerting an additional effort to restore the balance of body and mind, eating more healthily, etc.

Some of us only believe in God when we are in trouble. Others begin to behave kindlier toward others, become better listeners, and reflect on how they used to live. Illness, if we let it, can present us with an opportunity to take a good look at ourselves both mentally and physically, and to change our lifestyle as needed. However, most of us revert to our old selves and ways as soon as we are better. We forget what it was like when we were ill, we allow ourselves to be consumed by our egos again, and we live life in a way that induces imbalance, only listening half-heartedly to others' advice.

When we are healthy, we are reluctant to examine our essential parts or our inner self; our lives are busy, and we feel reasonably satisfied, overall. I am not knocking this—having peaceful energy within is key to maintaining balance. However, this is not the same as encountering the truth. To live without becoming aware is to remain ignorant. Also, to live is to experience changes, and there are some changes for which we are given no time to prepare. Think of the typhoon that washes everything away with savage force—if we were to experience such ferocity, we would find it very hard to get back on our feet. If only the typhoon would learn to destroy the bad, giving the good a polish before allowing clear weather to return. It is imperative that we keep our body and mind balanced at all times, so we can remain calm, whatever happens. If we are calm, we can treat illness and misfortune as pathways toward growth, in the direction of truth.

I would think that most of us have been on the receiving end of some sort of religious instruction, at one time or another—lessons about heaven and hell, etc. The usual intent of such lessons is to regulate our actions through an appeal to morality: do not steal, do not kill, do not mistreat others, etc.; in other words, do not let your energies flow in a negative direction. Nevertheless, we have feelings of anger and jealousy in our minds, which have accumulated through acts of karma and as the result of past lives. Even though these feelings may not overtly manifest, we carry them inside ourselves as a kind of inner complaint. If these feelings excessively accumulate, they can disrupt the mind's functioning and even cause us physical harm. So, please, try to increase your awareness of how your mind and body operate. Try to evolve your consciousness. Experience the truth and, ultimately, the divine.

Strengthen the mind through meditation

We live our lives wondering where we stand, in terms of superiority or inferiority, by comparing ourselves against others. We find it gratifying to feel superior, and we aspire toward it.

We tend to use external criteria to judge superiority or inferiority—we envy a person who is pretty, has a nice figure, is wealthy, lives in a nice house, is well educated, enjoys good social standing, etc. Our ego is stirred by these triggers. Many of us put effort into our appearance and work hard in pursuit of positions and titles. External comparisons are easy to make, and what is "better" is easily discerned. "You look great!" we say. But, as far as the effort to make our mind more attractive goes, it is lamentably rare for anyone to exclaim, "How beautiful your mind is!"

Alas, the inner self is rarely remarked upon from outside, and, once we have become used to being complimented on our appearance and other visible attributes, and we in turn are in the habit of complimenting others in this way, it can be quite difficult to recognize that there is value in being beautiful inside, too.

If you have read this far, I have no doubt that you are able to examine your inner self, and that you have chosen to live a positive life. By doing so, not only will you waste less energy, you will also acquire energy by using your mind positively. Again, the way to make this happen is to meditate. The more you meditate, the more peaceful your mind will be. To transform your inner self in this way is, to my mind, our most valuable act as human beings. It is an individualized act, yes; but, since ego is removed, it is an extremely unpretentious one—all the more so as it cannot be detected from outside. By removing attachments, our character transforms, and we become more at ease. This in itself is valuable progress. The evolution of your consciousness is a source of peace to those around, and, as a result, is linked to the evolution of all human beings.

Sometimes I am approached by those who seek to surprise others by meditation—or, I should say, by acquiring special skills through meditation. I have been asked whether meditation is a means of acquiring supernatural powers: Can we, for example, fly through the air while meditating in a seated position? The strict answer is yes— there are those who have been able to strengthen certain energies by controlling them. There are those who can rip a telephone book in half with their bare hands, those who can pull a truck with their teeth, etc. Often, such feats require entering into a trance state. However, it is possible to disrupt your overall balance by using these powers; it is not our purpose, as people, to acquire such traits. It is the responsibility of us all to practice with the right motivations; we ought not to train our inner self with the egotistical purpose of wanting to impress or control others.

Tap into wellness by maintaining bodily balance

What do we think of when we think of boosting power—an athlete? It is not uncommon for those who play sports to train and to build their muscles. Through training, an athlete's muscular glands become thicker; their muscles grow so that they become stronger. However, athletes need to be careful because, if their muscles grow too much, they become hard, like armor. Also, developing your muscles without strengthening your internal organs can create problems. Certain types of meditation, and the asana pose from the secret Himalayan teachings, are effective at training internal organs since they penetrate and stimulate the organs as well. You can certainly tone your muscles through weight training, but this doesn't strengthen what's inside. Just as muscles become strengthened the

Be born again with an original soul, in which desire, anger, and suffering have disappeared more you use them correctly, so too the mind becomes stronger and healthier the more you use it. In any case, why use the strengthened body to satisfy the overly inflated ego? In order to advance your mind, to balance and strengthen it, it is important to relax it as well as use it. To do this, you need to concentrate on a target that makes the mind feel at ease, and not be distracted by anything extraneous. This can gradually change into meditation.

Once you reach a state of mindlessness through meditation, your ability to concentrate is increased. Your idle thoughts diminish, and your level of understanding deepens. This understanding is important: it is not only the understanding in the sense of reading something and increasing knowledge; it is increased understanding in the experiential realm, as well as that of the senses.

We feel insecure when we don't understand things; we become anxious when we don't know what lies ahead. When a white cloth suddenly flashes across the eyes of a small child, the child may be frightened, mistaking it for a ghost. When the child looks again and realizes it is just a white sheet, they feel relieved. The child is seeing correctly, through awareness and realization. When we remove clouds from our minds through meditation, we get better at judging matters correctly. The more we understand and are able to judge correctly—without being deluded by preconceived notions—the better we are able to live at ease. We become stronger—in the true sense of the word—when we feel at ease. We gain strength as we move from ignorance to understanding, through increasing confidence. To understand is to see with a pure, unbiased mind, to judge correctly without being manipulated by our own obsessions or the opinions of others. The mind in its meditative state is innocent and free of prejudice.

The importance of being filled with deep love

I am sure you are familiar with the phrase, "Love conquers all." When we are filled with love, our hearts become strong. Love is synonymous with trust: deep trust causes positive energy to flow, and anything negative—such as doubt or anxiety—to melt away. When you meditate, it is advisable to target something constant, such as love of the universe or an everlasting eternity at the root, rather than focusing on changing targets. It is best to trust a high-dimensional existence that links to existence at the source as well as your own self. Continuing to meditate requires determination—the willpower known as *sankalpa* in the vocabulary of the secret Himalayan teachings. This derives from trust and your power of concentration. It is also important to pay attention to your body—it ought to be well balanced. Overdeveloped muscles aren't necessary; what's needed are balance, flexibility, and nimbleness.

There are quite a few people who live to a ripe old age even though they seem to be in poor health and get sick often. Such people regain their health by learning through illness, as they cleanse themselves and reclaim their balance over and over. People who brag about never catching a cold are usually quickly disheartened when they do eventually get sick and tend to give up rather than fight their illness. It can be dangerous to relax too much, by placing excessive confidence in the belief that you are well and strong. People who do so rarely take the time they need for their bodies to recover, which only makes their situation worse. We must all try to avoid placing too much confidence in ourselves through ignorance alone. Do what you can to become familiar with your body's condition; try to maintain balance, be healthy in both body and mind, and use your energies well.

Huge differences between those who meditate and those who don't

The energy generated through meditation can be thought of as a kind of light. It has the power to heal and can be directed toward specific people. However, if this is done too much, the mind gets worn out. A true practitioner is free of all obsessions; when their level of meditation deepens, they will become one with the universe. You will find that it is not necessary to consider whether or not particular thoughts should be discarded; obsessiveness will disappear of its own accord as you continue to meditate. This doesn't mean that you become passive and lethargic; you simply let go of everything and assume an open attitude. You look at things without being stoic.

Of course, as you fill with energy and your inner self becomes enriched, you will begin to realize what's important. That rare view you encounter on your travels, that item you have always wanted—you will realize nothing compares with the inner journey. To discover your true self is not to consume, and no joy can compare with the joy of discovering something new in yourself. No matter how wonderful and beautiful a particular thing may seem, you only feel the satisfaction of owning it for a moment, and, after that moment passes, you feel empty again. This means you have to select something else to fill the emptiness. This is how it goes with the satisfaction we derive from material goods. And let's not forget that there are many truly beautiful things around us—we simply tend to go about our lives without noticing them.

I should be clear, here, that the meditation I am referring to in this book is the various forms of meditation offered through the Anugraha Himalayan Samadhi Program, in which absolute happiness can be attained through training courses in the secret teachings of the Himalayan siddha masters, the goal of which is to become the best possible human being by acquiring enlighten-ment. The joy that you will feel as a result of practicing this meditation might be occasioned by something decid-edly minor—going outside again after an illness, or wa-tering plants in the garden. I assure you, there is joy to be found in such simple tasks.

Meditation will allow you to determine what is most important for you. You will be able to act with wisdom, and serenity of mind. For example, let's say you are think-ing about the tasks that await you at work tomorrow. You may feel rested and relaxed, but, if you are not in the habit of meditating, you will tend to focus on more worrisome matters—things you aren't so good at, matters you hav-en't taken care of, etc. Your mind is in full-functioning mode, which makes it harder for your body to rest. If you are in the habit of meditating, however, you will be able to focus your attention more creatively and devise better ways to succeed. Once your awareness develops further, you will be able to remain relaxed and firmly focused on the present.

CHAPTER TWO

Put Meditation Into Practice

1. Meditation is the cleansing of the mind

Attachments are only transitory

I am sure that, in your life up to now, you have tried hard. You have probably studied diligently, accumulated knowledge, and acquired skills to make yourself more adept at life. Perhaps, at times, you have learned the hard way, and taken some knocks in the process. You may well feel reasonably satisfied. We all enjoy eating delicious food, listening to good music, finally acquiring something we have long wanted to own. Our minds function smoothly, and time goes by. However, as I have mentioned, only one part of our mind is satisfied this way. It is a temporary satisfaction, which doesn't mean we are deeply fulfilled within. If such satisfactions remain our focus, we run the risk of coming to the end of our life without realizing what our inner voice has been asking.

Let me give you an example of obsessive mind at work. It often happens that, when we do a good deed for others, we unconsciously expect something in return—we instinctively expect others to be nicer because we did something for them, to be complimented because we were kind to them, acted in good faith, etc. Does this thought process issue from a genuine mind? No. It issues from an egotistical mind of desire. Furthermore, we tend to expect even more in return, when we treat others kindly. Our minds become hooked on satisfying this superficial desire. What solace can we hope to derive from such a perpetual demand? Also, when our minds are expecting something, it seems to be the most important thing in the world at that particular moment. We fixate on it, almost as if possessed, and if we can't get it, our minds become unsettled and distressed. Over time, our obsessions get pushed into the deepest corners of our minds, and our interests shift to the next target in line, even though we are unable to truly move forward, as the prior obsession is etched into our memories as karma, and contributes to our capacity to endlessly generate and replicate the same pattern of behavior.

Painstakingly release one by one

We tend to ignore our true selves and to take our obsessive minds at face value. But our true selves are part of everlasting existence—the source of existence where everything is created, another form of the divine. You have an alter ego, God, at your center—God, in this sense, meaning the supreme existence. The true way of life is not at the mercy of attachments or desires; it is the path toward experiencing the truth by encountering your true self. In order to attain this, you must cleanse your body and mind, deepen your awareness, and become genuine. You must align yourself with your center, which is linked to the truth. When you confront your inner self through meditation, you will see through your various obsessions, one by one. All you have to do is simply let them go; they will melt away naturally through meditation.

You cannot force this, through some sort of brainwashing. Urging yourself that "this is the way to think" tends not to work well, as you remain unchanged at your essential core. And unless you receive the grace (blessing) from a high-dimensional existence, you will lack the energy needed to transform. If your try to forcibly implement this change through so-called normal techniques, you will end up exhausted. Even certain methods that are commonly regarded as spiritual are anything but, in the fundamental sense. Sometimes people end up in bad situations, overly reinforcing and encumbering their minds, becoming oversensitive and overenergized, opening the door to yet more obsessions as a result. Don't give up. Don't overly rely on the pleasures of the senses. Don't allow you mind to become tainted by particular concepts or doctrines. Time passes quickly. All the more reason, then, to embark on the search for your true self.

Wisdom from samadhi is true wisdom derived from the existence at the source. It is the teaching of the Siddha masters who have transformed their lives through love and wisdom, and it is the path to meditation that will allow you to be fully here in the present. It is a rare path, and I aim to make it possible for you to encounter it.

Burn impurities of the mind

Laws of cause and effect apply to everything, and a good cause is essential to creating a good effect. However, it is possible to overemphasize this concept, and it can become burdensome to constantly be on the lookout, making sure we are only doing good deeds and thinking good thoughts. Tiredness results from the unhealthy convictions of the ego, even if its desires are pointing in a positive direction. Sometimes we act to defend ourselves unnecessarily, thereby creating additional problems for ourselves—I'm sure we have all experienced these kinds of situations. When we act, there is a result, which has consequences; is it better, then, simply to do nothing? It requires courage to put this into practice—to not plunge ahead, but, rather, to control our actions. This ability is imperative.

Perhaps you think that to act—or not act—in this way is foolish? In fact, we are exposed to such behavior every day. For example, we use the expression "my mind went blank" when we come across some shocking event; it indicates that our thoughts momentarily ceased, leaving us in an abstracted state of mind. When we need to protect our psyche, our automatic control mechanism kicks in as a self-defense device. This actually provides an important hint as to how we can better function in life. By putting the secret meditation techniques into practice, we can bring our minds to a state of perfect serenity. Having done this, we can control our thoughts and actions far more effectively. I think of meditation as the anti-aging method bar none—one that keeps us truly beautiful while also enhancing our immunity to disease.

How to throw away and release trash

Our memories and thoughts accumulate over time. They exist within us and are also recorded in cosmic space. The thoughts and memories that result from our actions in life form the base from which we continue to judge, compare, deplore, and obsess. Negative thoughts function as shackles on the mind, restricting it from exercising its full potential. Most of these, I am sorry to say, are unnecessary trash. This may seem harsh, but from the point of view of a calm and pure mind, the active mind seems noisy indeed, and it is useful to take out the trash and keep the mind clean. It would be great to clean the mind all in one go, but unfortunately this is not possible—that is, you can only do so through the wisdom and love of a samadhi Yogi who is well versed in the mind and body. Without that help, such a drastic cleanup is impossible. When a room is a total mess, we don't clean it up by striking a match and setting fire to its contents.

To clean up effectively, we start by clearing things away in a systematic fashion. Some of these items might cause us to reminisce: "Ah, yes, I remember this!" Other items might be associated with quite bitter memories, so that we wish to be rid of them as soon as possible. Perhaps we might even enjoy watching these things smolder in the flames. When our trash has been burned, a wide-open space is left in its place. Affection and kindness are more likely to issue from a pure mind, while anger and jealousy are purified. In our "room" that is now neat and tidy, it is so much easier for creativity to emerge. Don't you feel excited, just thinking about it?

I want you to clean your mind for your own sake, and I urge you to set aside time for yourself. You will feel so much more at ease when your body and mind have been returned to an orderly state. You will feel refreshed, invigorated, and newly creative. Your views will broaden, and your life will feel much freer; goodness will naturally come your way. So, too, you will instinctively perform good actions for others—there will be no external pressure or force. The stage is thus being set in preparation for surpassing all: being liberated from your body and mind, becoming your true self, being regenerated and reborn. This is spiritual awakening.

Abilities increase when the inner self is cleansed

What I can do to help you is to change you from within. This is not a matter of giving you temporary instructions or a superficial method of how to succeed in life. I will introduce you to a path that can't be accessed in any other way, and which certainly can't be bought with money.

It is true that human culture has developed and that we appear to have become more knowledgeable in certain areas. However, our improved skill at eradicating pain does not in itself mean we have made any progress in our minds. Are we free of anxiety, desire, hatred? Do people no longer get sick? Those who encounter the path via the secret teachings are truly blessed, as only those who appreciate its true value *will* encounter it. This is not what is usually meant by a learning opportunity. The secret teachings in no way resemble how-to seminars. We may possibly learn from the success stories of those who have become multimillionaires, etc., but there is no guarantee that we will meet with the same success simply by emulating their actions. Every person's karma (memories of actions and their results, from past lives up to the present) is different, which means our actions will have different results, even if they bear superficial resemblances. And besides, how important is it to aim for success when you consider our true worth and value as human beings?

Training the mind in a significant way

Having all of your faults pointed out to you will only succeed in making you feel unmotivated and discouraged. Also, while it is possible to change our habits on the surface, we remain programmed, deep down, to do the same things; we need to maintain our balance from within. The secret teachings will allow you to maintain balance while developing self-awareness, so you can focus on the important business of how to live your life. Do we wish merely to copy those who are successful? It is almost impossible to watch others without judging them, which only compromises our own ability to make proper choices. It is time, then, to advance our meditation. Provided our inside is clean and tidy, we will be able to maintain balance from our center rather than through past habits. Health, tranquility, and wisdom can be ours. Creativity, too, is an aid to purification. By making a habit of meditating, all areas of your life will improve, and talents you don't even know you possess will awaken after lying dormant for too long.

Create a space of stillness within you

Practice "giving" things you cherish

I often tell people to "become mindless." It is an odd request, I know, and I am not surprised to often be asked, "How can I achieve a state of mindlessness?" This is hard to answer because there isn't just one answer. Also, this is something you come to know by realizing it yourself, and it takes time. Try to avoid asking such questions, if you can—the very act of asking questions requires the mind to work, thereby removing it still further from mindlessness. Your mind works harder as it tries to understand; answers are acquired in the process of meditation.

Our competitive society teaches us to judge everything: this is good, this is not so good, etc. We are accustomed to making comparisons and distinguishing between good and bad. In the early stages of meditation, as you begin to look at your inner self, it is common to feel surprised and perhaps even distressed by the negativity you discover in yourself. As you continue to meditate, you will see various things within yourself, such as the ego. Negative aspects of self are not a reason for disappointment or dismay; creating turmoil within will only exhaust you. In fact, feeling bewildered and distressed is a sign that karma is being purified: you are emptying as things gush out and melt away. Over time, as the space of stillness within you grows, you will begin to be annoyed by the mind that criticizes and denies you. And then, when you desire to make the mind still, to achieve the state of mindlessness, you will know how to achieve it.

Mindlessness takes time, but the Anugraha Himalayan Samadhi Program purifies and melts karma quickly, allowing you to achieve mindlessness by expeditiously purifying the clouded mind. Let's look at the mind a little more closely. You have to accept yourself as you are, if you are to achieve mindlessness. Forgive yourself, along with everything about you—all of our minds are obsessed with trivial matters at times. Accept this and reflect on it. Accept that your actions take place out in the open and take a hard look at them.

Though it's not easy to accept your own actions under normal situations, consciously focus your attention there. The eyes and ears as the sensory organs are attached to your face on the outside, and so you are aware of external events. We often view the world unintentionally, but depending on who you are, your level of awareness differs in terms of how much you perceive. People are prone to notice things that are occurring on the outside but are not apt to notice what's happening inside, and so it would be advisable to become aware of your own actions and/or thoughts.

The mind's awareness through the act of "giving"

Desires accompany all actions. For example, let's assume there are two rice cakes of varying sizes in front of you, and the other person picked the one that is bigger. Do you feel, "That person picked the bigger one, and it is unfair?" If you're on a diet, you may feel relieved thinking, "Oh, good the other person picked the bigger one, and I am happy to end up with the smaller one." Or, rather, you may think, "I wish I could have eaten the bigger one," if you are hungry.

We exhibit a certain level of emotions even when speaking of rice cakes depending on our conditions. And, you may feel, "Ah, I hate it. I have this greedy desire in me, and it's ugly." Or, you may not care either way and just gobble the rice cake.

From this point on, let us learn how to become aware of these workings of the mind. To become aware of them is your learning process.

In doing so, you will truly feel, "It was good to have given the bigger one to the other person," if it comes from love as you exert compassion without being at the mercy

To give, to devote, to share

of your desires. That's because you will be able to cultivate the feeling of "giving" by evolving your mind to a higher level.

In general, there are times when you feel good in "giving" and other times when you feel sad. When you watch children, you can clearly tell the difference. For example, children give items they don't care about freely one after the other, but they will tenaciously guard items they cherish. They are reluctant to lend them also.

And here in order to cultivate the feeling of giving, you will practice how you would feel when you give away something dear to your heart. You will envision an image of your giving away something that you most cherish rather than giving some items you don't need or care about. And, you can raise the level of this act of giving depending on how you feel at the time.

For example, if you felt, "What a waste. It was a loss," this shows your level is still low, and so you would then envision giving away some item that is not the most precious but next to the most precious.

In this way, you will imagine yourself parting with cherished items one after the other by gradually modulating the level of practice. All parting may be described as "giving."

And at the end, you will practice letting go of your life as the most precious of all the things. It's crucial to assume a frame of mind in Samadhi training founded on a strong determination to let go of your own life based on this type of trust.

However, generally, because we experience fear when we think of losing our lives, it's quite challenging to envision casting off our lives. We all experience in life many changes, parting with people that are dear to us and loss of valuable items. And so we practice "giving" them away. Discarding items you don't need is obvious and is an act that makes you feel good. Then you can evolve this into giving away something precious, or to which you are devoted.

Speaking of devotion, people in India frequently dedicate offerings. An offering is an act of "giving" and is one of dedication. Through offerings, you can let go of your obsessive mind within—the mind of desires—and obtain sanctity. Through the act of sharing and devoting, you can drop your own mind of desires, remove attachments of the mind, empty them, get closer to the essence, and become gradually happy.

This in turn is a good deed where attachments of the mind are removed all at once, as you advance purification through an action engaged from outside. This is referred to as exoteric teaching. It is defined as the teaching that is visible to the eye. Surprisingly, by advancing good deeds, the mind becomes serene from the outside action and at the same time removes obsessions and/or attachments on the inside, generating good meditation.

In addition, meditation is an ascetic training of the inner self through practice. It's called esoteric teaching compared to the exoteric teaching. This is an act where you are connected to the Master through trust, receiving graces of an unseen existence, dropping your entire ego in an instance, resigning and becoming empty through surrender and by dedicating everything. Ultimately, what it means to surrender is to dedicate everything to your true self where you let go of various thoughts and obsessions and become obedient to the existence at the source.

By meditating in this way, you will be able to give and dedicate, and if you were able to realize, "It's good to give, share and dedicate." You can then express this feeling in your everyday life.

If you notice that you are obsessed with something, it's proof that you are saddled with desires. And in order to unburden what you have burdened yourself with, you must become unselfish.

When you realize it, please practice "giving," "dedicating," and "sharing." It's a good idea to proceed with good deeds then. In doing so, you will be able to meditate at a higher-quality level.

Meditation is a cleanup of the mind

Through the Anugraha Himalayan Samadhi Program's kriya meditation, as well as kripa (Anugraha through a disciple) and Anugraha diksha, your mind can attain the serenity of a polished mirror. Yet remember: only true masters can guide you into deep meditation, and for your part you must realize what your mind and body are and be able to control them. You will come to accept your obsessions, understand them, transcend them, and let them go. This can occur quickly under the guidance of a master.

In the process of living, our minds get hurt; we have cause to suppress anger, endure sadness, and continue to live with buried emotions from the past. Many of our desires remain unfulfilled, and feelings of frustration and disappointment linger in the form of memories and stress—an unwelcome residue in the mind. Even this residue goes through changes and can become stimulated through human relationships which cause the ego to surge in self-defense when it experiences conflict. In life, this process is repeated again and again; it is endless, unless we become awakened. When you receive the graces of the secret teachings, you will relax as your karma emerges and safely disappears through the release process. As your meditation proceeds, you will be able to examine your inner self more closely. Once the room of your mind is cleaned and tidied, you may find that you are easily able to find answers to questions that had hitherto perplexed you. Your insight will deepen, and creativity and inspiration will be more readily available. Also, with your thoughts more organized, your efficiency will improve significantly. With an open and flexible mind, there is nothing to fear from external stimuli; you will welcome people into your life, as if your mind is saying to them, "Please come in!"

The key to quieting the dust

What would happen if we didn't clean the room of our mind—if, that is, we lived without meditating? Our minds may well contain many wonderful things, but it is hard to locate them when its room is in disarray. We may well be sitting on a goldmine, but even our best ideas will struggle to let themselves be known, if they lack sufficient space. Also, the act of cleaning inevitably stirs up dust, and we might be surprised as to what is revealed. Your master will teach you how to suck up this dust, almost as if you are a vacuum cleaner. By trusting the master and connecting to the source, you can clean safely, and your mind will be prevented from playing tricks on you. Cleaning too quickly can be risky—a sudden change to your mental environment can be unnerving. It is said that animals and fish which develop under laboratory conditions have less immunity than those that live in the wild. A certain level of impurity is necessary as it helps develop resistance. The key is always to clean with awareness and wisdom—entrust yourself to the guidance of a Siddha master and move forward with your meditation at the right pace. Maintain a comfortable environment for yourself and clean little by little, always with awareness and acceptance.

We have become accustomed to placing importance on manners, outward demeanor, niceties of speech, etc. What's more important, as we have discussed, is the inner self, which necessarily goes unnoticed. The inner self is purified through trust and belief in all-knowing existence. The secret teachings of the Himalayan Siddha masters will allow you to purify distortions of the self and transform your mind.

2. What Can One Gain from Meditation?

Acquire intuition and inspiration

Once you get into the habit of meditating, you will be able to deal with things promptly and effectively. You will judge matters accurately. Without meditation to aid you, however, you will continue to struggle; your mind will remain in its confused state and you might find yourself at a loss, being simultaneously pulled in one direction and pushed in another. This can only result in stress. These days cars have so-called navigation systems that guide you from your current location to your destination. Some of the more efficient systems will even point out the most efficient route, based on road conditions, traffic congestion, etc. Like such systems, those who meditate regularly will intuitively know which path works best for them, and even be able to take effective shortcuts through heavy traffic.

What happens if you don't meditate, feel exhausted and confused in life, and are on the receiving end of an overwhelming amount of information? This is like looking at a tree without being able to see the surrounding forest. Some people may find life to be more exciting this way— they may think that facing unexpected obstacles makes them feel more alive. To my mind, however, this way of life feels like butting your head against the same tree—or like walking along with a heavy load on your back and chains around your feet. Clearly, if we continue to do this, the body will eventually become exhausted. Even a trained athlete weakens if they are forced to jump the same hurdles repeatedly. Unfortunately, many of us waste our energy in this way, albeit unconsciously. Through Himalayan Siddha meditation, not only can you live more easily, you can also tap into additional energy elsewhere.

Do not try to use the mind too much

Meditation is a training to "transcend death"

Once you are awakened through meditation, you will be able to see how your mind works. You will know your ego—and your egoism—well. You will see why you became angry over something minor, why you wasted energy on something trivial. The obsessions of your ego, generated by all the dusty memories of various past experiences—karma, in other words—will melt away. You will become more considerate, forgiving, and patient. Furthermore, as your conscious mind advances, you will be able to assume the ability of selecting the most suitable way to act in a given situation. Your understanding of the mind and its workings will deepen, and you will be able to purify your own reactions. Anxiety and panic will become less frequent visitors; if you become ill, you will be able to make decisions calmly, and recognize that the illness is an opportunity to regain balance. Once your wisdom is in fully working order, you will no longer fear death. The Himalayan Siddha meditation that leads you to samadhi will guide you to this ultimate state of consciousness; it is truly "a training to transcend death."

In the language of Buddhism, the path to enlightenment is called *kuju-metsudo*, or the Way Leading to the Cessation of Suffering. The cause of suffering is the mind. You may think that meditation is somehow akin to sleep—it is true that, at a glance, a sleeping person appears to be filled with stillness and peace. However, even when we are sleeping, we are not truly at rest. The deeper realm of our subconscious is still active: we have dreams, talk in our sleep, toss and turn in bed, etc. This may be a result of releasing tension accumulated during the day, purifying thoughts related to it, and so on. There are certain habits of the body and mind we cannot stop, even if we are aware of and understand them; the mind will always react to external stimuli, which in turn stirs up emotions. Karma accumulates in this way; it is exhibited in our actions and released through sublimation. In this way, the acts of living and dying are repeated over and over through many lives. While we are asleep, karma remains in a confused state, essentially unchanged. A purifying process aiming at samadhi is very different; here, everything is still, and oneness is attained.

A confused mind can be cleansed of past traumas and various memories of experiences from past lives through the workshops of the secret Himalayan teachings, through Anugraha diksha and samskara diksha. Our emotions and thoughts, our surface reactions to things—these all have causes deep within; our assumptions and impressions from past experiences create tendencies in us. They can be removed through increased understanding or by being filled with love from within, and this can be achieved through the master's wisdom and love. Your awareness will be enhanced with blessings as your purification deepens.

You no longer feel blue when you meditate

We are obsessed with the outside world. We are always wondering what others think of us, while our reactive minds go about their business, busily making comparisons. Before we go out, we groom ourselves, decide what to wear, fix our hair in certain style, etc. Now, I am not suggesting we pay no attention to our appearance, merely that the world within us cannot be seen with the eye. A person whose inner world is fulfilled wears a gentle, contented expression and exudes an aura of happiness. Sometimes a person who has money, a house, a successful career, etc., seems dissatisfied and exudes an abrasive energy—they appear to be deeply unfulfilled within. To put it simply, they have remained at the level of the ego and have never encountered their true selves. The rich energy that exists deep inside them does not spring forth, but instead is dissipated, leaving them empty and lonely. Plus, there is always the risk that external wealth will simply disappear one day, whereas no one can rob you of inner abundance. It is also impossible to take external wealth with you when you die, whereas inner abundance remains with you in the form of the astral body, where the innermost soul resides.

To return home after a long trip always makes us feel relieved, no matter how enjoyable the trip was. We relax, release the tension that accumulated over the trip, and feel glad to be back home. These feelings—ease, relaxation—exist deep within us. But where, exactly? In our physical bodies? In our minds? Or beyond them? What type of life should we lead, if we want true richness to flow from within? To explore these questions is to pursue a way of living where true growth is attained. To live as before, attaching or accumulating external elements in order to feel momentarily happy at the level of the ego, is to create confusion which inevitably leads to conflict. A new way of living is to link directly to the truth.

We feel anxious in life as our minds try to anticipate the future: What if I am involved in an accident? What if I get sick and can't work? Our imaginations only amplify our concerns—even before any problems arise, we are exhausted by the various what-ifs. In fact, just as the proverb says, "Well prepared means no worries." Some degree of preparation is always a good thing. However, being consumed by worry doesn't solve anything—it simply denies your mind from functioning more usefully. Try to relax and see the whole; make use of creative means. It is perfectly acceptable to use the means and let God give the blessings. Problems don't get solved through worry; through trust and relaxation, your inner wisdom can spring forth, and good results will inevitably follow.

Also, when your actions bring joy to others and you act kindly toward others simply for the sake of doing so, the

Transcend the mind, time and space, and death

cycle of good energy you generate becomes stronger, and, through a curious mechanism, you will find that you no longer get depressed. You will understand that everything is a learning process; you will feel grateful for it, and all that constrained you will disappear.

Meditation can be practiced till death

Our competitive society has numerous values and rules, and we all face problems, large and small. Many people commit suicide because they no longer feel able to cope— no doubt they think it a relief to end everything, to forget everything through death. I question this, however.

By cutting life short in this way, the memory of pain is retained in the astral body, the body of energy that resides within the body, and the memory continues to live in the endless process of rebirth. The pain caused by the act of suicide then impacts not only the person's family, but also casts a shadow—in the form of suffering—on the evolution of rebirths. I admit to holding the view that suicide should never be encouraged or allowed. There is hope. There is salvation. Everyone has the ability to access profound wisdom, to understand all, and to change fate by coming into contact with it. This is done through meditation.

Even if you feel happy in the here and now, you can meditate for the future of your children, to acquire wisdom, be empowered by love, and furthermore to make others happy. If you feel so worn down by life that you have contemplated suicide, you will be able to calm your feelings through meditation. By meditating, you can release the mind of its obsessions and quiet it down. Meditation opens up a way of life where you are not at the mercy of your desires but can live fully in the present moment and observe without judging. It is an ascetic training in which, as we have discussed, you will eventually surpass the mind, time and space, and death.

To become empty does not mean to become dumb. Rather, you will become aware of the fact that desires of the body and mind generate suffering, that egoism and ignorance create suffering. And you will know at the deep level that your true self exists beyond egoism. By continuing with the workshops and various forms of meditation, you can advance awareness of mind and continue to purify it. In addition, through Anugraha kriya, your energies will be purified and controlled, and your entire body will be filled with energy. Samadhi Yogis know this energy well and can control it.

Through meditation, we can purify our memories up to now, understand suffering, and change animosity to forgiveness. By continuing through the Anugraha workshops and practicing various forms of meditation, you will be able to evolve your thoughts and connect to the new wisdom by eliminating what is unnecessary or superfluous for good. You will be introduced to all of the necessary training and meditation techniques in the Anugraha Himalayan Samadhi Program. The program offers a basic course, an advanced course, short training camps, and regular training camps, which all proceed in a step-by-step approach.

Various stages of meditation

After you have been meditating for a while, you will begin to understand a lot of things inside you. Your head will become clear and wisdom will spring forth. The pressure on your brain will ease and blood flow will improve, making you feel more energetic and improving your cognitive and bodily functions. You will know acceptance and awaken from within. You will also have a chance to reflect on various events and to repair the past, if necessary, deepening your awareness through purification and letting go. Someone once told me this: "I thought that, if I meditated, I would be enlightened right away by becoming empty. It didn't happen like that." This is because hardly anyone starts with a clean mind and body at the beginning—most of us have little idea as to what lurks inside ourselves. It can happen, however, through the blessings of the secret Himalayan teachings. You can even be enlightened right away, provided you surrender all of yourself immediately with a genuine faith and trust in accepting all the blessings. In general, though, our egos tend to be enlarged with all kinds of knowledge, thoughts, and memories, and our minds are usually confused.

Many things come to the surface during the purification process; different memories rush in, but they are all from the past, and can be purged. Thoughts come to the surface that are not truly you, but which simply belong to you— they have been holding you prisoner, in fact. You will let go of the way of life that entailed hiding behind psychological armor; you will become open, pleasant, and kind.

Most of us feel uneasy about the physical changes associated with the aging process. But, by becoming aware of these changes, we realize just how important it is to satisfy the inside instead of taking care of the outside. And those whose inner selves shine are also wonderfully radiant on the outside and exude an aura of profound contentment—a kind of glow. By meditating, you advance purification of the body and mind, and by connecting to the life force at its source, you develop an intrinsic beauty from the inside. In this way, you can be assured of evolving yourself, no matter what your physical age. It would be challenging, of course, to take up sports at the age of eighty, but honing one's skills by connecting to the power source and accumulating energy to the body, mind, and soul really is the best way of living an active and happy life.

I sympathize with those who have to make hard decisions on a daily basis: premiers, presidents, and prime ministers, as well as corporate leaders. But life without a title, lived away from the public eye, can be just as hard. This is why I recommend the path of truth and enlightenment to all: it is blissful to know one's true mission in life, to encounter life's source, and to live an enriched and truly fulfilling life.

Meditation changes life to joy

It used to be commonly assumed that those who succeed in life possess high IQs (Intelligence Quotients). These days, however, EQs (Emotional Quotients) are considered more important. The important thing for us to note is that both a person's IQ and EQ have been observed to increase as a result of meditation. Many people have corroborated these findings, and it does indeed seem to be the case that, through meditation, people get smarter. I myself am not overly concerned about how many hours I sleep and how much work I get done. I understand that most regular people benefit from routines, but a Samadhi Yogi who has transcended time and space does not require much sleep and tends to be minimally restricted by their environment. I maintain myself at samadhi level, and when I meditate I get rid of tiredness right away.

Those who aren't in the habit of meditating usually suffer from accumulated fatigue and disrupted balance, and this is usually the gateway to illness. It is common, for example, for people in middle age or older to train through physical exercise, obsessing over their physique while never attending to their level of consciousness. The risk here is that, by pushing themselves more and more, the mind hardens, and energy levels deplete rather than refresh. Exercise is good, of course, but it is also decidedly basic. By meditating, you can experience a profound stillness that allows you to shed your obsessions. When the mind relaxes, you are better able to live free of pain and suffering. Therefore, if you exercise, you should meditate at the same time. In this way, you will be able to balance your life, evolving your conscious mind by recharging your energy from a profound place at all times.

It is human nature to forget what pain is like as soon as we feel better. If your condition improves through meditation, it is important to continue to meditate rather than settle for your present improved condition, for this is the beginning of true purification. It is vital you make the commitment to continuing to meditate. Those who meditate habitually are not concerned with trivial matters, and so they make people around them feel relaxed—their very presence can make those around them heal. You too can do this; your existence can bring courage and help to others. Because you meditate, those around you feel the richness and warmth you exude. As your wave motion is transmitted to those around you, they too become peaceful and enriched. Isn't this, in itself, a significant contribution to society?

I am in earnest when I beg you to accept the notion that you are not here merely to satisfy your worldly desires and pleasure your senses. Even so, I do not go so far as to condemn the way you choose to live. All I ask is that you spare a little time in the morning and evening for meditation. Once it becomes part of your daily routine, your life will start to overflow with love, and you will impart warmth and kindness to others. Your life will be one of joy, and you will communicate this joy to those around you.

3. Live Beautifully Beyond the Age of One Hundred

The mind becomes one through mantra's waves

Light was born from the existence at the source of the universe; then sound came into being. The wave motion of sound created words; then thoughts were created. The wave motion of sound is linked to the source. The wave motion of sound definitely purifies your body and mind from deep within. You can feel this by expanding the sound's waves internally. Thoughts subside and stillness starts to fill you; your inner self begins to fill with kindness, love, and peace. The wave motions of sound and its mysterious pulsations are specific energies that reside within—energies that correspond to the existence at the source referred to as the divine. You focus your conscious self on the wave motions to be in tune with them.

The pulsations of sound align and purify the areas of your mind, working to maintain balance by melting toxins from the mind. The pulsations themselves are not the mind, but by harnessing them you can purify the mind and use the pulsations as a vehicle that transports you to a realm beyond. Of course, music is comprised of sounds, but developing the ear by listening to music is different from taking a journey inside the soul. Listening to a piece of music, you feel the composer's intentions as well as his karma—it has the feeling of the person who created it. Though music may at times have a healing effect, it can also result in a hardening of thought and imagination.

What is the wave motion that can purify your own karma? The first step is to solidify trust through prayer and meditation. Then you are bestowed with a sacred sound pulsation through the secret teachings of the Himalayan Siddha masters. This pulsation is not created artificially but derived intrinsically as a gift from God; it is a sacred pulsation that is empowered, intoned, and purified by a true samadhi master. As I have mentioned, this is not something you can acquire by reading a book or two. Meditation through sacred sound pulsations is called samadhi meditation. Through the energy initiation rite called samadhi diksha, and initiation into samadhi meditation, you will receive your sound pulsation. This sacred pulsation purifies your karma from deep within. When you use it, your conscious mind will gradually broaden as if it is a river flowing into the sea—the sea in which you will attain the realm of oneness.

Know science of the mind and surpass work-related stress and illness

We live bounded by time, at all times. Ours is an era in which we are expected to manage time well; wasting time is frowned upon and tasks are expected to be completed according to deadlines. We are constantly under pressure, needing to finish this and that—it's no wonder we become neurotic about time. Efficiency is important, of course, but we shouldn't let ourselves become haunted. Sometimes people work so hard, their health suffers—one person succumbs to a subarachnoid hemorrhage; another suffers from cerebral thrombosis. This is usually a result of their energy balance going awry. If you feel you are blessed with a healthy body and a strong mind that can withstand challenges, if you feel full of vitality and ambition, and believe yourself to be living a life of comfort and happiness, I urge you to take a moment in which to focus on your inner conscious mind—simply focus on your conscious mind to see if anything may be brewing inside.

Even if you have a healthy body and a strong mind, and feel blessed with good fortune, you may not know your true self or have acquired the wisdom of truth from deep within. The highest purpose in life is to become a complete person with an evolved wisdom who is filled with benevolence. I earnestly wish you to spend the life you have been given by doing all you can to live an authentic life. Take the time to look inward: focus on your conscious mind, on your inner self, and become aware of the more precious things.

Meditation organizes your inner self. It purifies you, allowing you to access the original, pure, and innocent self where everything is revealed. Therefore, there is a world of difference between the way life is approached by those who meditate regularly and those who don't. Those who don't meditate exert themselves unnecessarily, eventually becoming exhausted. Those who do meditate are clear-headed and live with boundless consciousness; even as they advance in age, they continue to help those around them. They live in such a way that they are able to celebrate getting older. Indeed, according to recent studies, meditation is even effective in rejuvenating the brain.

Proof of relaxation to fall asleep during meditation

Let me, here, respond to some of the questions I have received from readers and students. Firstly: "How do you spend the time during samadhi? Aren't you sitting in the same position for as long as four days? Is it possible to die from suffocation?" Samadhi is the ultimate meditative state. It transcends time and space, allowing your mind and body to become one with your true self and the existence at the source of the universe. I have been underground for four days on samadhi, and I came back. You transcend your body as it is cleansed, just as the mind's function disappears as it is purified. Your bodily functions cease, as do the workings of your internal organs. Of course, nothing is eaten, and there is no digestion or elimination. Though you don't stop breathing, it stops on its own. You arrive at your true self, exceed the silver lining, experience God, and become the existence at the source of creation. You surpass time and stay in the present moment without past or future. Four days seem like an instant.

If you engage in profound meditation, you too will have a samadhi-like experience briefly; however, in order for that to happen, you must start by purifying everything first, and you must feel confidence and trust. Karma is also a factor. If some training has already been done through past lives, you will be eager to seek something more substantive. By meeting the Samadhi Yogis of the Himalayas, you will be able to meditate deeply and come much closer to the possibility of your own samadhi.

Stillness and infinite love abide deep within you

Let's move on to another question: "I understand that you were able to do it, but isn't it dangerous for others to try to attain samadhi?" Clearly it is dangerous to go underground and have the opening sealed above you. A normal person, even if they meditate, will continue to breathe and end up using all the available oxygen. The likely scenario is that they will die of suffocation due to carbon dioxide poisoning. In India, some practitioners who have trained quite intensively have attempted samadhi and died in the process. Training, purifying the mind and body, transcending the mind, and obtaining the best conscious state usually requires many past lives. It takes many hours of preparation to understand the mind, remove attachments, purify all, and maintain balance. A true master can reveal the path, but the path only opens by trusting, surrendering, and continuing to meditate diligently. Through the daily practice of meditation, you will acquire profound relaxation and be reinvigorated by life's force. A long life and full rejuvenation will be yours. Speaking for myself, I often fall asleep before I know it. Falling asleep while meditating helps to purify you of profound fatigue and can also be regarded as proof that you are truly relaxed. At the same time, it means there is still work to be done—body and mind are not yet completely purified. Overly excited nerves need to relax and rest. When you awake from meditation, you will feel refreshed, and as you continue to practice, your cleansing will advance and your ability to rest will improve. Through the secret teachings of kriya, dark energies called *tamas* will be quickly purified, opening the way for transformation.

4. One Definitely Can Change Through a Journey of the Mind Called Meditation

Meditation is an "interesting" journey of the mind

Here is another question: "I started meditating several years ago, and I tend to fall asleep right away. When I asked what I could do about this I was told that my temperament wasn't suited to meditation. I was somehow convinced by this, but listening to you makes me think I was wrong. I think meditation is good for me, and I would at least like to do it over the weekend, if not every day. What can you suggest for someone like me—is there some secret I should be aware of?" I think it is important to decide on a certain established method, because meditating without being sure of what you are doing can make you anxious. Also, as discussed earlier, the mind can throw up unexpected things in the course of meditation, and this can be off-putting. It is essential to have a teacher who can provide you with a meditation technique that matches your temperament. Also—and I must say this—I don't believe there is a temperament that is unsuited to meditation. The fact that you fall asleep means only that you need sleep, and sleep during meditation is not the same as nighttime sleep. Your teacher's guidance will help you to become more alert, and, as you rid yourself of impurities, you will find that you don't need to sleep as much. Also, even though meditation is an inward journey, the views it affords are hardly without interest. As you continue toward your inner self, those around you will register your transformation—you may strike others as having become substantially different. My aim is to guide you toward the genuine you, so that you can acquire happiness and radiance, and discover the path to true selfhood and enlightenment.

Receive an initiation

Here is another fairly common question: "Should I meditate in the morning, and will burning incense help me to get further, or should I simply close my eyes? I would like to go deeper."

The important thing, always, is to be guided by a Siddha master. By merely sitting down, a smooth transformation of inner energy cannot be generated, and it will be very hard for you to enjoy your meditation. Even basic meditation is powerful and natural and should cause you to feel very much at ease. In order to improve your meditation, the most important thing is to try to maintain a certain way of thinking: try not to be swayed by the workings of the mind, and especially by any negative thoughts. A positive, grateful attitude will help you shore up your energy, rather than deplete it. Even a slight modification of thinking such as this can do much to aid your meditation practice. As long as you received an initiation into the secret teachings at the outset, you will be able to meditate smoothly and productively. If you are under my guidance, you will first receive prayers which will deepen trust by connecting to a high-dimensional existence. Then, stresses and distortions from past lives will be cleansed through initiation with a high-dimensional energy called diksha. With balance maintained and energy purified, you can awaken your inner self to harness the energy of the existence at the source. This is the point at which the secret technique using wave motions is imparted. Through this, you will be able to purify safely and naturally. This is what samadhi meditation involves. You will be required to take a vow to establish trust.

Later on in your training, the secret of Siddha kriya meditation will be imparted, to provide high-quality purification. Through the blessing of your master's Anugraha, you will be able to open the invisible door to your innermost self. Since the environment in which you meditate is important, you should select a place where you feel comfortable, in a room where you feel relaxed. Also, it is a good idea to decide on a time to meditate in advance—when you continue to meditate at the same time every day, you will somehow be facing in the right direction instinctively when that time comes. It is always a good idea to make meditation a habit.

In addition, meditation conducted under the guidance of a master will deepen more quickly due to assistance in the purification process from what we can call group consciousness or group mind.

Reclaim your original self

Let's move on to the next question: "Does your initiation involve particular steps? Can I get into the meditative state merely by closing my eyes?" Yes, there are different steps that correspond to each level within the secret Himalayan teachings. This meditation practice is a discipline for life, and it is better to advance one step at a time by passing through the stages. Some people think that closing the eyes is all that is required, and that the guidance of a master is unnecessary. The obvious response to this is that, if it were possible to meditate meaningfully in this way, there ought to be many people in the world who have attained an enlightened state. Also, if you meditate superficially in this way, you will find it very hard not to be distracted by trivial and mundane thoughts (it is also easy to become bored and lose interest). By advancing your practice under a master's guidance you will come to understand what you have amassed inside, and what you can usefully discard. What's more, you will do so safely, without risk. A master's guidance is crucial because cleaning up the mind is not a straightforward matter; strong thoughts can work like magnets within us, pulling us in all sorts of directions and generating confusion as a result. The further you advance, the greater the risks, without the guidance of a master.

As we have discussed, the culture of the Indian people is naturally endorsed by their faith; it is no surprise that India is where meditation was born. In India, great emphasis is placed on connecting practitioners with the appropriate master—this is essential if the high-order energies are to be linked. In order to assure this, the meditation of prayer is received first, after which you proceed by accepting diksha. You will continue to purify with safe wave motions, and to progress through further stages, as needed and as they are revealed to you. Through easy-to-follow workshops, and under the protection of Anugraha, you will purify your mind and deepen your awareness. At the same time, by putting the secret kriya technique into practice, you will acquire inner strength which will enable you to remove stress and fatigue, as your energy center is cleansed and becomes awakened. In addition to our basic and advanced courses, we also offer short and weeklong training camps.

Once the secret teachings have been revealed to you, you will undergo a complete transformation and be reborn with quite extraordinary abilities. Merely "sitting" does not produce this profound change—you have to actively seek transformation, and you need a master's guidance for that. By working with me, for example, you will be able to rid yourself of stress and exhaustion. This valuable lesson took me many decades to learn, and I regard it as my duty to share what I have learned with others. The secret teachings of the Himalayan Siddha masters comprise a rich life science that is truly awe-inspiring. The path to enlightenment, the true path to happiness, the path to transformation and going beyond—these high-level attainments usually require many past lives to accomplish. But, through the secret teachings, they can be yours. With my many years of practical experience, I can guide you to true happiness by opening the door to your inner journey—indeed, it is my earnest desire that you acquire genuine happiness and achieve real growth.

Just as I was able to change, you can change too

Here is another typical question: "My image of meditation involves someone sitting cross-legged in a kind of Zen position. What do people do if they go numb or get pins and needles?" I am sure we have all experienced this, but I assure you that pain or numbness in the feet, knees, or hips is due to lack of balance in the body, which you then focus attention on. No one who meditates with me ever suffers from such problems, even if they are meditating for the first time. The transformed body and mind of a Samadhi Yogi such as myself goes beyond our traditional notions of body and mind to become existence at the source; from there, a very strong willpower called sankalpa cleanses the energies of those around me, transforming them instantly. Because of this, even if you are meditating for the first time, you will be able to sit for many hours without any problems. The intricate energies I first became aware of in the Himalayas will be transmitted to you through me—this is called Anugraha. The greater the trust of the person who is receiving it, the greater the force with which they receive it. The secret teachings will align your energies, which also promotes your ability to sit for a long time without discomfort. Even people who have not previously been able to sit without pain find that they are able to do so with me; they are astonished, in fact, at how quickly they transform. Again, this is thanks to the grace of Anugraha. When you experience meditation at a profound level, everything will be filled with love, and you will feel as if you are melting toward God. You will train at a high level with extraordinary speed and make progress

Create the same state inside of our minds as the Mother Nature of the Himalayas

that would otherwise take some twenty to thirty years to achieve. I truly want as many people as possible to transform and become happy, and this is why I have chosen to share what I have learned. Also, I believe I was chosen specially to encounter the secret Himalayan teachings and to discover the truth by attaining samadhi. I want to share this gift, rather than merely remark that I was fortunate to be chosen. In the past, these teachings have only been made available to royalty and high-ranking officials. It is time for that to change. The secret teachings are finally being opened up to everyone through me.

As I say, I am not from India, but, nevertheless, I was chosen, and I was able to graciously and humbly proceed along the path that was revealed to me. Now, I want to share this with you. I think we, as humans, need to revive our spirituality, and the secret teachings present us with the opportunity to evolve spiritually in the truest and most meaningful sense. Can we revive our trust and belief in the existence of something larger than ourselves, something that can't be seen by the eye?

MEDITATION OF SIGHS

When something upsetting happens to us, or we feel blue, we often let out a moan or groan: "ooh," "aah," etc. We often moan when we are in pain. When we are glued to our desks for many hours and want to take a break, we make a similar sound. You can let such a sound form the basis of a simple meditation: simply breathe out, "whew," gently and gracefully.

CHAPTER THREE

The Path to Samadhi

1. The Path Involving Twists and Turns

My youth was spent battling tuberculosis

As I have said, samadhi is the ultimate stage in Yoga training; it is the genuine awareness that can only be acquired through profound meditation. All of the sensory organs, body, and mind are controlled, death is transcended, and space and time turn into light, which then becomes one with the existence of creation at the source and God. In other words, enlightenment occurs within samadhi. Samadhi is also referred to as moksha, nirvana, and supreme enlightenment. A person who has attained samadhi suffers no pain whatsoever and is filled with joy, love, power, and wisdom.

In India, samadhi is regarded as the highest state a person's consciousness can be evolved to; those who have attained it are treated with great respect. Their exquisite energies cleanse the magnetic field of the planet and its people. There are saints called Himalayan Siddhas who live deep in the isolated mountains, where they have been immersed in samadhi for many years. Twenty million ascetics aspire to this state, having renounced the world in their quest for truth and enlightenment.

My own path, until I encountered this training, was full of twists and turns. I am envious of you, as you hold this book in your hands: your path is sure to be quicker and easier than mine was! Let me, here, tell you a little more about myself. As a little girl, it was my habit to pursue everything in earnest. I liked to know how things were made and how they worked; I asked "why" all the time and was always creative. I like to think that I was good, obedient, and hardworking. I think, as I got older, I felt the increasing need to be serious-minded, and tried to behave as though I was older than I was. I think I was probably too serious, and a little uptight.

When I was fully grown, I went to sign up for a swimming class, thinking I should exercise more. I was told to have a physical checkup, which included a chest X-ray. To my shock and dismay, it was discovered that my lungs were covered with tuberculosis germs—the disease had already progressed to quite an advanced stage. It is true that I used to have coughing fits in the middle of singing a song, and often felt that something wasn't quite right. Also, my father died of tuberculosis when I was one and a half years old; it should have occurred to me that I was at risk. There was a long time during which I couldn't do what I wanted—my body simply wasn't up to it. I was forced to take complete bed rest, despite being so young.

Illness as catalyst

With my illness as a catalyst, I began to find out more about how the body and mind work. I spent many days reading everything I could find. It was during this time that I decided to really study yoga. I had been interested in yoga before, and had done yoga exercises, but it felt a little too hard on my body—of course, I didn't know my body had already been weakened by tuberculosis. I still think yoga has a lot to do with developing my hardworking nature.

Even after I was cured of the disease, I was extremely afraid of moving my body for a while. Recuperating tuberculosis patients need complete rest and my life was very restricted—I wasn't even supposed to talk much, let alone move my body vigorously. During my long convalescence I became so anxious about moving just a little, or taking a breath, that my doctor finally suggested I resume normal life. This is when I took up yoga again. As my strength and confidence returned and it became clear I was going to make a full recovery, I decided to aim as high as I could in yoga. Eventually, through the recommendations of others, I was invited to teach yoga at a local cultural center.

Now that I had the responsibility of teaching yoga, I realized that it was my responsibility to enhance my own level by studying more and putting in more effort. I began to research various forms of psychotherapy and to study psychology.

Desire to develop great instructors

I continued to teach yoga at the cultural center while studying psychology and healing. The number of students increased every year, as did the number of classes offered at the center, until eventually I was one of around twenty instructors. At the beginning I went to each of the classes to continue to provide additional instruction, but as the number of classes increased, it began to take too much of a toll on my body. I realized I needed to spend less time exerting myself and more time developing the other instructors. Some students requested to work with me and me alone, making quite flattering complaints that they wanted to learn directly from me. The staff at the center pleaded with me to do something about the situation, worried the center would be adversely affected. I felt caught in the middle, wanting to help but simply unable to do all that was being asked of me.

Then it occurred to me that, after people have spent time and energy loudly asserting their opinions, and as hurtful as those opinions might be, they will in time give up. I decided to keep going and to endure as much as I could. I continued to study, to teach at the center, and to train the other instructors. There was no business model to appeal to, no "this is how it ought to be" to emulate. I groped along in the relative dark, trying my best to map out my own path. My sense, now, is that my conviction got me through: I was determined to make my students as healthy in body and mind as I could, and to train the other instructors so that they too would become strong leaders and excellent teachers.

Desire to encounter a great master

Although things were going quite smoothly, I felt that something wasn't quite right. I also realized I was beginning to resent spending so much of my time training the other instructors. Yes, the instructors were learning and advancing, but what was I doing? I felt as though I was stagnating, and that I needed to grow too, if I was to do a good job. I thought that I needed to develop myself more, and that this would somehow be conveyed—quite naturally—to the instructors and students.

There was another aspect to this. While the instructors were definitely developing satisfactorily in terms of technique, something internal seemed to be amiss. I would always tell them to be grateful, to keep an open mind, etc., but I reminded myself of a dog barking in the distance, and I couldn't help feeling my advice was not being put into practice. As I thought about why this might be, I came to the realization that you can't simply be told to do internal things, things that aren't visible; you have to see the need to do them on your own, and this is how to begin to change. I felt that, if I was able to elevate myself to a higher level, I would be better able to guide others correctly.

From that moment on, I was single-minded in my pursuit of the truth. I looked for a great teacher because I had so many questions about life. I continued to study and began Zen meditation on my own. I became healthier and achieved a certain level of success. I should, I suppose, have felt a certain level of fulfillment and happiness. And yet my journey continued. I continued to ask "why," but, even though I had an enormous amount of information at my fingertips, I still felt baffled. This situation lasted for quite a while. Then, one day, completely out of the blue, a godsend of an opportunity presented itself: I was asked by a TV station to assist in an event involving a Siddha master from India.

Various therapy experiences in the United States

The task I was requested to perform was to assist Pilot Babaji, a Himalayan master, to perform an underground samadhi in Japan. Pilot Babaji, one of the most renowned Himalayan masters of recent times, was then beginning to attract a lot of attention. He had already conducted samadhis that were open to the public, as part of the global movement for world peace. Now he was to conduct one in Japan. The underground samadhi that Babaji conducts is one of the most challenging practices there is. He is completely denied surface-level contact during the four days he spends in the underground cave.

The TV station was at a loss as to how to effectively present this great event. I was asked to lend my support simply because I was beginning to be recognized as one of the pioneers of yoga in Japan. When the samadhi had been successfully completed, Pilot Babaji turned to me and asked, "Would you like to train by coming to Himalaya?" This was both an unreal invitation and a dream come true. Up until then, I had visited India more or less annually in my twenties and thirties, to study various forms of yoga by visiting training centers there. I had also visited the United States on numerous occasions, keen to study various forms of psychotherapy and the New Age healing techniques that were then very popular. These techniques were imported to Japan and these days the spiritual boom is a thriving industry, but back then, over thirty years ago, it was was quite unheard of to be interested in these pursuits. Though my English was hardly proficient, I was quite courageous by nature and had no qualms about traveling. I was able to participate in various psychotherapy sessions and spiritual seminars, and even had the good fortune to visit the home of one of the therapists.

Many of the spiritual movements in the United States at that time consisted of mix-and-match yoga parts which were picked because they were approachable, then blended to create a version of yoga that was more commercial in form. There was nothing holistic about these adaptations, and there was no question of attaining truth by becoming your true self—if anything, what movement there was took place in the opposite direction. And so, no matter what I did or where I went, I was unable to find satisfactory answers to my questions.

2. Training in the Himalayas

To the sacred place, Himalaya, of my yearning

The request from the TV station, then, could not have been better timed. I did not hesitate to accept Pilot Baba-ji's invitation. I had first read about the Himalayas in my teens, and by the time I reached my thirties my yearning to go there was strong indeed. Why was I drawn there so strongly? I can't think of a particular reason, aside from my hunger for genuine experience.

I had of course already visited some of the sacred sites in India: Sacred Place in the foothills of Rishikesh, Utta-arakashi, and, further inland, Gangotri. Now, the place I longed to visit was much further into the mountains—the unexplored region of Pindari. Pindari is situated next to Kailash, Tibet, where you cross the Himalayas. It exists on the precipice of danger. Huge rocks are strewn about, and it is especially vulnerable to avalanches in high winds or during storms. I was told that to journey there as a woman alone was certain death. Friends pleaded with me tearfully to abandon the idea of going there. The Himalayas are sacred mountains. Once you cross over them, there is a place called Kailash, the sacred place in Tibet where Shiva is said to reside. Many regions across the Himalayas are still referred to as unexplored territories, and it is here that the Siddha masters live, fully immersed in samadhi.

And so, I was given the opportunity to visit this extraordinary region. I went to the Himalayas and I trained in the unexplored regions. Much of my training was done in the Pindari Glacier region. I visited Bandrinath and Gangotri and journeyed further into the inner regions of Nandabahn, Tapovan, Kailash, and Ladakh. I continued to meditate as I traversed this terrain. Here I would like to mention an experience I had when I was meditating in the Pindari valley. As I was meditating there one day, I entered into a profound stillness by shedding all of my thoughts. My body began to shake, and I had no idea what was happening. The shaking continued for a long time; it felt as if it was occurring beyond my body and mind, and as though my body and mind were numb. I wasn't controlling it, and yet it was happening naturally. I saw that my body was on the outside. Then my body died, transcending pain and sensation, and I continued to go further, beyond body and mind. I stayed sitting for many hours without moving. Then I came back. I had experienced samadhi.

This was at the beginning of my experiences in the Himalayas. It was an experience I had never had before. The masters who were training near me confirmed that what I had experienced was samadhi. All of me changed, and I was transformed. Since then, I have repeated this type of training and have experienced samadhi sometimes for several hours and sometimes for several days. I have also trained myself in underground samadhi, and, with the support of a master who also acted as a witness, I have immersed myself in a four-day samadhi. Now, I am always with samadhi.

Journey to Kailash

Since then, my trips to the Himalayas have continued every year. The holy Mount Kailash that rises above the Himalayan mountain range is a sacred mountain which has drawn many faith seekers and ascetics. It is shaped like Mount Fuji, with an elevation of about 6,600 meters, and is where Hindus, the followers of Bön, and Tibetan Buddhist monks come on pilgrimage. Once they arrive at the base of Kailash, they make a circle around it on foot for three days and three nights without stopping; this is called *parikarma* (circumambulation of sacred places). Pilgrims from Tibet make the round by engaging in an act of prayer called *gotai-tochi* (a prostration in which hands, legs, and head are pressed to the ground). By pressing your body to the ground in gotai-tochi a sense of unity with the earth is created, along with a sense of oneness with the deities as you peel your egotism away and empty the mind in advance of charging it with energy. Even the base of the mountain sits at an elevation of 4,500 meters. This is a life or death pilgrimage.

There are two routes to Kailash. One is to enter through Tibet, and the other is to come from the Indian side; however, the route from India is indescribably harsh, and you have to continue to walk the path, with no cars passing by, for one whole month if you wish to cross the border. The danger is great. Indian pilgrims start their journey on this side, and some die each year due to the extremely harsh conditions. When I was there, I witnessed such a tragedy—four young people died. However, Indian families who are deeply devout accept such deaths as fortunate, as dying in the holy land is considered to be the quickest path to heaven. The faithful make this pilgrimage in order to purify their minds and bodies where the deities reside. It is an unbelievably harsh journey, with reduced oxygen at that altitude; it helps to be trained in yoga as well as devout.

I made the journey to Mount Kailash three times, in 1990, 1996, and 2001. On the last of these visits, I brought my disciples from Japan. We flew from Katmandu to Lhasa and drove to the foot of the mountain, after which we walked on foot for three days. Even the capital of Tibet, Lhasa, is more than 3,600 meters above sea level—the height of Mount Fuji—and making the pilgrimage requires walking on foot in terrain at a height of more than 5,000 meters. The samadhi Yogi group I was guiding was able to complete the pilgrimage safely, protected as we were by the blessings of Himalaya.

Mount Kailash is a dangerous place, but there is an increasing number of people who wish to make a pilgrimage to this holy mountain, even if it means risking their lives. Today, we see people accessing the remoter regions of the Himalayas from the Indian side; the government, even, has begun to promote the pilgrimage, with the result that it has become a fairly popular endeavor.

When I first visited the Himalayas at Pilot Babaji's invitation, however, it was an unknown territory, almost as if it belonged to the earliest days of our planet. There were hardly any visitors there then. Huge rocks lay all around, and we trudged along a path which was little more than an animal trail. The threat of falling rocks was ever-present. Even losing your footing a little would result in falling into the mountain stream hundreds of meters below. I still consider my annual pilgrimage to the Himalayas to be part of my training. Danger could be anywhere, and I feel protected by God in the Himalayas.

There is something precious in the Himalayas that we have lost

You must wonder why I choose to visit such a dangerous place every year. While I can't give you one clear reason, I do know that it is my karma, and that I wanted to encounter truth by spreading the serenity, grandeur, and deep love of the Himalayas. I felt that I had to defy danger in order to discover the truth.

How can I describe to you the blue skies over the Himalayas? They are endlessly blue, transparent and clear, and how free the birds seem that fly around there! The huge rocks are more grounded now, remaining calmly and firmly in place even when storms hit or winds blow. How serene are those rocks that nestle in the stillness! The river of the Himalayas carries snow-melted water and joins with the headstream of the Ganges. Downstream, the sacred Ganges is expansive like an ocean; Indian people bathe in it to cool their hot bodies—the climate teaches them the preciousness of water. The river flows powerfully, with calmness and innocence, bestowing its blessings on the earth. The clear blue skies, unbounded freedom, a calm, composed stillness, a love that only gives . . . all are to be found in the Himalayas. Here, Mother Nature reminds us of the precious things we have lost.

Look at the stressful lives we lead! No wonder we are so full of anxiety and confusion. Nonetheless, I think it is helpful to at least be aware of our stresses, and not to give up, not to forget that there are ways in which we can release ourselves from them. If you experience the stillness of the Himalayas, a stillness that goes beyond your inner self, you will conquer your stresses. In the process, you will realize how much stress you were regularly exposed to, and you will be aghast. Then you will realize just how precious what's inside you really is. But to actually visit the Himalayas is no easy task for most of us. How, then,

Perfectly clear blue skies, Freedom bound by none, Calm stillness, Only a giving love… All of these reside in the Himalayas

can we experience the stillness of this sacred region? What can we do to recreate the Himalayas' Mother Nature within ourselves?

My mission is to make people happy

In the Himalayas, there are samadhi Yogis—that is, Himalayan Siddha masters—who have entered samadhi for decades by transcending the body, mind, and death. However, these Yogis rarely visit our world. When I visited the holy land, I was lucky enough to meet Pilot Babaji's teacher, Guru-Hari Babaji, who still lives in an unexplored area of the Himalayas. He gave me diksha and blessings. The day before I was to make my descent from the mountain, Hari Babaji said to me, "I want you to elevate the spirits of the Japanese people. Convey the message of spirituality that goes beyond the mind. Communicate the love of the Himalayas. Make them happy. You have the power to do so." Having received the blessings of Hari Babaji, I continued with my training. I was then able to meet the great master of Hari Babaji, Ottah Babaji. Back then, I was very aware of my limitations as a teacher, and Ottah Babaji must have sensed what I was thinking; he said to me, "It is your responsibility to make people happy. Communicate the nobleness of samadhi to everyone. Convey the truth and awaken them. Lead people to true happiness. Guide them through enlightenment."

This amount of responsibility seemed a tall order indeed for someone as inexperienced as me. Nevertheless, to hear these words from such a noble master was very humbling. I began to think that it was indeed my mission—a call of duty that went beyond the responsibilities of the individual. At that precise moment, I realized that I was feeling completely relaxed. I was entirely immersed in and at one with Mother Nature of the Himalayas. I began to think about those who were awaiting my return back in

Japan, and I realized that I was wishing with great sincerity for them to be feeling as relaxed as I felt, wishing too that they be given the chance to encounter the supreme existence and truth.

After returning from the Himalayas, I felt relaxed, blissful, and truly fulfilled. I also felt that I had to convey this feeling to everyone—a feeling of relaxation and joy that is as transparent as the skies of the Himalayas, as free as the birds, as powerful as the river, and as immobile as the rocks. But how best to impart this message? How best to put it into practice? I continued to ponder this. I have now performed a total of eighteen public samadhis in India, their purpose being to share love and peace, and to send the message of truth to the peoples of the world. We all have tremendous sacred power inside us; we are all beings that are filled with love and peace. I truly believe that samadhi Yogis have the power to heal people, cleanse the environment, and guide people to samadhi. And I am convinced that I can impart true happiness, evolution of consciousness, and the path to samadhi through the eight steps of Yoga, by introducing you to the wisdom of the Himalayan Siddha masters, through the Anugraha Himalayan Samadhi Program.

3. Eight steps to samadhi

First step: Forbidding discipline

There is the teaching of Hasshodo (the Eightfold Path) in Buddhism. This is a training that recommends eight essential practices if one is to enter into nirvana. The eight practices are: the right way to see and think, the right words (no lies), right actions, right living, right effort, right feeling (in other words, right care), and right mental concentration. This path is the correct way (dharma) and true teachings of Buddha. In Buddha's lifetime, religious training in India was centered on asceticism, but Buddha reacted against this, preaching a middle course which avoided both austerity and hedonism, encouraging his followers to practice the eight steps.

The eight steps of Yoga that I am about to introduce to you relate to Buddha's Eightfold Path, but they are more concerned with transformation (Buddha also visited the Himalayan masters and explored different methods of releasing suffering). We can attain samadhi by proceeding with these eight steps. But first let's ask ourselves, who are we, really? We think our bodies are us, and we are also our minds; but are these really what and who we are? We think we know our own minds, but is this really our authentic self? We will never know our authentic selves unless we train and acquire true freedom.

We contaminate ourselves with desires and our ignorance about how to use our bodies and minds correctly causes us to accumulate stress. One action, based on our desires, causes the next action, and this chain reaction continues, with the results of our actions accumulating as karma. There is the guideline called *yama* which helps us acquire a correct—moral—frame of mind. Based on it, we can prevent ourselves from contaminating body and mind. This is referred to as "forbidding discipline" and what it forbids is our desires.

So, what is forbidden? According to yama, we must not use violence; we must not steal other's property; we must not lie; we must not engage in too much sex; and we must not eat or drink excessively. By forbidding certain actions in this way, the desires of the mind can be controlled, and our right actions also serve as a cautionary example to others. These types of teachings are put into practice through thoughts, actions, and words. According to the secret teachings of the Himalayan Siddha masters, our actions live on as memories, stored in our minds and bodies along with whatever energies were connected to them.

Also, our motives for taking these actions derive from an area where the past is stored—this is commonly referred to as the law of karma. The forbidding discipline of yama shows us how we ought to live, what we ought to do to generate good results, and what we should do to live a life that is not contaminated or at the mercy of superficial motives. We discipline ourselves so that we don't rush to gratify our desires or act out of ignorance or anger. If we do good deeds, use kind thoughts and words, the same will come back to us from others around us.

However, our minds cause us to suffer and fret, and if you have a strong ego, conforming to discipline, even if self-imposed, is by no means easy. And the memories of our experiences from past lives are deeply engraved in our minds, forming a template which predisposes our future actions. For example, we hate others simply to protect ourselves, triggered by energies from the past. We all get jealous and scared; we get carried away and feel the impulse to strike someone; we get angry when our ego is hurt. The ego really is troublesome! So, what can we do with this mind of ours? One idea is to always try to think, in a given situation, of the complete opposite. In other words, instead of hating, you forgive; instead of getting angry, you allow yourself to forgive. By forgiving, you can control your desires. However, we are human, and we have a proclivity to do things we know aren't good, but which we can't stop ourselves from doing. It is crucial to examine these thoughts and habits. What are we trying to defend? By proactively enhancing your awareness through the Anugraha Himalayan Samadhi Program, you will become aware of your obsessions and be able to cleanse each level of your mind and body.

Through Anugraha, the high-level blessing which Himalayan Siddha masters bestow, transformation occurs internally, smoothly removing clouds from the mind. In the absence of accumulated karma, there is no need to restrict our actions through forbidding discipline. Why?

Your consciousness goes through a transformation

Because we have become filled with love, full of respect for ourselves and for others.

Second step: Recommending discipline

Next comes the "recommending lesson." By practicing good deeds, you can increase positive energies within, which can then be shifted in more creative directions. There is a discipline in which people cleanse themselves. Many Indian people bathe in the Ganges to cleanse themselves, and their faith in the river is so powerful that it has the effect of purifying their souls as well. The Japanese have a passion for cleanliness and enjoy taking baths; being clean makes their minds feel good and refreshed as well.

We make our surroundings neat and tidy by cleaning and throwing things away. Our minds feel refreshed when we rid them of unnecessary clutter. We can also groom ourselves. Yogis are so proficient at this that they can clean the stomach, intestines, and nose. There is also a practice of purifying through *qi* and the breath, and we can purify our bodies though our choice of what foods pass through them. Eating natural foods and avoiding processed foods aids purification.

However, if these positive techniques are adopted by the mind alone, there is a danger of taking them to an extreme and accepting nothing less. This can lead to the mind developing an excessive sense of justice, so that judging others becomes an obsessive act, and we become overly prejudiced. It is always best to undertake such practices under the right guidance, so we don't overly pressure ourselves into acting in a certain way. And so, the mind is cleaned at the same time as the body is groomed. The mind can be purified in various ways; the first step is to assume a grateful, pure, and loving attitude, free of prejudice.

We can also cleanse our words, by trying not to utter words that hurt and insult others; instead, we should try to speak with love, using beautiful words and heartfelt phrases to encourage others at all times. Beautiful acts, words, and thoughts help to purify the mind. Beautiful acts, such as doing good deeds for others without expecting anything in return, help to increase positive energies referred to as merits. All of this can be done in daily life. In addition, there is a teaching called *tapas* in which you purify the mind and body by practicing asceticism. You can select an action and perform it in order to foster spiritual power by absorbing the desires of the body and mind. Such actions might include not talking wildly or even choosing to remain silent. At times, you can affect healing or work toward enlightenment by controlling your release of energy this way.

We can also control our eating by ridding ourselves of the desire to eat as much as we want. In India there are many restrictions with regard to food; certain religious ceremonies only allow the eating of fruit, and all monks are vegetarians. You might choose to deny yourself specific foods as a way of deepening your faith. By doing so, you can cleanse your internal organs and purify your mind at the same time. Another form of ascetic training involves pain endurance, such as tolerating extremes of heat or cold. Also, the mind can be purified by listening to lectures on truth and memorizing sacred words. It is crucial to believe in the Siddah masters as high-dimensional existences, or free deities.

As I have mentioned, your initiation onto the spiritual path will take the form of diksha (energy to cleanse karma from past lives), which you will receive from a Siddha master. Through this, you will connect to the supreme existence and receive sound waves to purify the mind and body, and to protect yourself. By connecting to the master and reciting that sound, your spirituality will be enhanced, and your mind will be safely cleaned and purified. This will then empower your meditation, enabling you to gradually revive your authentic self. This is where enlightenment occurs. Acceptance is also important—that is, assuming an attitude of being satisfied in the present moment. The mind will never rest while it is seeking this or that desire. Instead of feeling that you don't have this and that, try to be satisfied with what you do have, and aim to start in a better direction from that point on. This also links with purification of the mind. Through the Anugraha Himalayan Samadhi Program, you can advance your awareness and accomplish true growth as you continue through the stages of the program. Proceed gradually, if you prefer, fostering trust as you go, or aim straight at enlightenment on the most expedited path. The Anugraha Himalayan Samadhi Program will accommodate you, whatever your preference may be, but you should know that the evolving of consciousness is a lifelong path. The path to enlightenment normally requires many lives to be lived over and over. There is no need to overexert yourself through either yama (forbidding discipline) or niyama (recommending discipline); through the Anugraha Himalayan Samadhi Program, all eight steps are covered, and you will be guided toward a more enriched life. Simply perform the steps unselfishly and leave the rest up to God.

Third step: Asana (adjust the body)

The next step is called *asana* and concerns adjusting the body so that you can meditate comfortably and healthily. When your body is out of balance, your energy flow becomes distorted. The stresses of everyday life accumulate in our bodies, causing us to become unbalanced. And most people use their bodies in a distorted fashion depending on their inherent dispositions. As a result of work, lifestyle, and karma from past lives, the body develops certain propensities. Some of us use our brains more, some of us use particular organs more than others, etc. Those who tend to eat a lot, for example, are overloading their organs. Those who drink excessively are putting stress on their liver. Those who play golf frequently are bending and twisting their bodies in ways that may cause problems. Plus, experiences of past injury and surgery stay in the body and mind, influencing our present energies. Those who work in the same posture for long periods of time run the risk of creating deviations because energies do not spread through the body equally. Such bodily deviations eventually create distortions in the mind. When yoga was in its infancy, life wasn't as convenient as it is now, and we used to move our bodies more. Despite this increased convenience, however, we seem to be under more stress than ever before. If your training is to be truly transformative, you must be conscious of posture and balance.

It is crucial to build a body shape free of distortions and to develop the proper mindset, so that energies flow evenly throughout the body. For this to be realized, we need to work on our posture so we can sit properly, having removed blockages from the body. From here, we can work on restoring and improving the balance of our nerves and muscles. There are eighty-four basic asana poses in yoga, and some two thousand variations on these. The basic forms are copies of shapes assumed by various animals that are vital for their survival. Through training using these, we can increase the freedom and naturalness of our bodies. I have thoroughly researched these poses, and, based on them, devised an osteopathy movement called *pranadi* and a yoga dance. The body carries out actions at the behest of the mind, and the mind is connected to existence at the creative source. We work to purify the mind and body from deep within by first connecting there. Asana itself is easy to follow and practice, but it is vital that, from the outset, we use our minds properly.

This is where Anugraha comes in—the high-order energies of God's graces which are born directly from existence at the source. The first initiation you will receive is diksha, through which you will be able to maintain balance while also cleansing deep within, purifying your mind and body. Then, a high-order energy called kripa will be imparted. Depending on your individual needs, there will be a loosening effect internally—through connecting to Anugraha—and asana will be achieved without effort. Asana will be put into practice with the guidance of a master who will help you realize what's inherent within. In this way, you will eradicate distortions of the body and align the flow of energies. The true purpose of yoga is to encounter truth, which means to become a complete human being; for this, you will practice profound meditation in order to encounter your genuine self and enter further into samadhi.

With asana, both what you do and how you do it are important, and, in addition to the training itself, awareness is crucial. Listen to the advice of your master; it will help to increase your understanding, especially of deeper and more profound meanings. For our purposes, asana can be regarded as a preparation phase, something that enhances meditation rather than simply improving health by maintaining balance. It is a way of training the body so that you can better look within while sitting. You can progress by connecting to the power of Anugraha, without being obsessed with the physical body.

I should perhaps say that I believe those who have already achieved some success in society are already proficient in mental concentration, either through karma, strong willpower, or natural talent. Such people appear to be taking care of themselves without taking time out of their busy daily schedules, but, in truth, few of them are truly taking care of themselves. On the contrary, it often becomes all too easy for them to become arrogant by placing too much confidence in their strong minds. Although they are skilled at using knowledge acquired through experience in their line of work, they usually know little or nothing about the existence that allows them to live, or who they truly are, or the sacred existence and truth that is invisible to the eye. Deep down, and regardless of their level of awareness, they are anxious about whether this really is all there is to life. It is crucial to wish for completing one's life with wide-open eyes.

The esoteric wisdom gained from Himalayan Siddha Yoga guides you gently so you can solve problems—even difficult ones—at the root. This is not to say that this wisdom is merely a matter of teaching solutions; rather, it allows the mind and body to maintain the balance necessary for intrinsically solving problems and deepening awareness. Solving problems can be done using particular techniques, but wisdom springs forth at the samadhi level, where you will see how things are structured and what actions you can most usefully take. In addition, through the high-order energy initiations of Anugraha and kripa diksha, you can cleanse the mind and revitalize your energy from deep within, eradicating distortions and melting away problems in the process. A person with wisdom is someone who can remove any obsessions about their body. By releasing themselves from these obsessions, they become blessed with a body and mind free of all cloudiness. If you too come to possess such a body and mind, you will start to demonstrate your abilities to the maximum. And not only will you be able to solve your own issues; your positive actions will also enrich the store of human nature.

Fourth step: Pranayama (breathing method to control the mind)

The word *yoga* means harmony and balance. Nature does a very good job of maintaining balance, but still there are times when balance gets disrupted. When this happens, nature induces all kinds of events in an attempt to restore it; earthquakes and volcanic eruptions are examples of this: through them, the earth tries to restore its balance and regain stability. We are all children of nature, and we should take time to learn from the lessons nature gives us. By being aware, by harnessing the supreme existence through prayer, we do our best to maintain balance so that we can coexist happily with nature. Feelings of awe and appreciation in the face of nature can be useful catalysts.

Our bodies are born from existence at the creative source and, as such, function as microcosms of nature. It is always advisable, therefore, to pray and be grateful rather than distance oneself from nature in the name of vanity. However, unfortunately, most of us use our microcosms in distorted ways, filled as we are with many desires; some of our energies are excessive, while others are deficient. Our energies will not flow in a balanced way when they are skewed like this. In areas where energies are used a lot, or where there are obsessions, they can converge and become hardened, and strength in other areas decreases where energies become deficient. It is very important to maintain a well-balanced state if you are to rectify these disturbances.

I am sure that you have already devised your own creative methods to aid relaxation, and that you are in the habit of deploying various techniques. However, in order to maintain the balance of mind and body, and to align the balance of energies such that it restores your former state prior to any distortions, the best and quickest means is to diligently practice the eight steps of the Anugraha Himalayan Samadhi Program that I am discussing here. The program places you on the path to your true essence, rather than simply allowing you to maintain a superficial balance. We can become aware of our true selves by carrying on a dialogue with what is deep within us.

Our bodies are driven by our minds. The body moves because the mind thinks; it doesn't take action on its own. Because the mind thinks where to go, you take the action to go there, and because the mind thinks of wanting to eat something, you cook. In other words, the mind functions before the body moves. In this way, as long as the mind thinks proper thoughts, the body makes the corresponding right motions. However, the human mind is always obsessed with many things. Our minds go back and forth with these thoughts all year round. We tend not to focus too closely, but if we did, it might occur to us that the mind when it is preoccupied is never free. Our obsessions and interests shift, causing our minds to get stuck, which then inaugurates the endless process of doubting, vacillating, and judging. In this state, the mind can know no tranquility, and can never rest. It ranges likes against dislikes and is constantly shifting, which wears it out.

When the mind is obsessed with something, all of our energies pour there, and the mind acts with little regard for our actual intentions. For example, we drink too much despite knowing that drinking excessively is not healthy. Unable to stop while being well aware of the dangers is due to the mind's own rotation and the momentum of its own force. A superficial attempt to control it at the level of morality is no use—you can't defeat the desires and obsessions of the senses.

Secret of assuming "mushin," the state of having an empty mind

What can we do, then, to quieten our minds and stop them from being so active? The Himalayan Siddha masters know the mind's internal workings thoroughly and are able to conquer it. One way of doing so is to concentrate on a single area; alternatively, you can assume the state of mindlessness. You make the mind empty by making everything extinct, whereupon the functions of the mind cease. To empty one's mind may sound easy, but it is in fact quite challenging. Through receiving the blessings of the secret esoteric teachings, you will be able to use kriya to melt away any clouds from the mind at the source.

We think we know what our minds are up to, but we are unable to control them—our minds seem constantly to be planning ahead or consumed by obsessions from the past. We find it inordinately hard to stay in the present moment. We think we are in the present, but actually we are not. The mind is always wavering, either in the future or the past, and is disjointed as a result. Still, we have it in mind to do our best, and we have the ability to concentrate. This is admirable, no doubt, but we should remember that we find it easy to mistake as concentration what is actually an obsession resulting from working too hard. In other words, we think we can strengthen our minds by overexerting them. This in turn becomes a habit and we wind up obsessed with always having to be doing something, even when nothing is required of us.

As with the body, so too with the mind: it gets exhausted when it is overused. We pour our energies into obsessions, preconceived ideas that have accumulated over the years, value judgments, ambivalence and negative thoughts, and we create mental turmoil for ourselves. The mind that results from this tends to be quick to judge and is easily convinced to give up rather than go on. Or it prevents you from giving your all, because you are pre-occupied by insecurity, doubt, jealousy, anger, etc. What you need to do first is realize how much energy is wasted in this way. Then, you can start to make proper choices by becoming aware. You will no longer be swayed by unnecessary matters. You can empty your mind and become as pure and open-minded as a baby. Wisdom flows from an unbiased, empty mind.

We all want peace of mind; we all want to feel secure. I want you to advance in your cleansing and learn how to control your mind in order to reach enlightenment. To do this, you have to restore yourself to your original, balanced state. By making your mind empty, you will be able to use it more effectively, feeling secure without dispersing your energies unnecessarily. The secret teachings of the Himalayas include various techniques for this.

Know conditions of the mind through respiration

Let's learn how to breathe in order to control the mind. You can control the mind by controlling your breath, or *qi*. You will know your state of mind, based on your breathing. For example, if you are angry, you will probably be breathing hard. If you notice that you are breathing hard, please take a deep breath; by breathing deeply, you can correct your breathing and ease your anger. You can maintain a peaceful state of mind at all times by consciously controlling how you breathe.

Through breathing, you bring in oxygen as well as the life energy called prana. Prana exists in between the mind and the life existence at the source. Humans advance cleansing of the body and mind physiologically by supplying prana through breathing and maintaining their nervous systems in balance. You can purify the mind psychologically while also—by controlling your breathing—going back to the creative existence at the source. The breathing exercises will invigorate you internally. When this is done without the necessary knowledge, unwanted or unhelpful things can at times be awakened, which could harden the mind, should the mind choose to regard them as legitimate energies (or, we might say, supernatural powers). There are certainly cases where people have suffered unnecessarily at the mercy of such energies.

The breathing exercises appear easy on the surface because we are always breathing; but they involve the nervous system and physiology, as well as energy, psychology, and spirituality. It is crucial, therefore, to have the guidance of a master. The breathing exercises practiced by the Himalayan Siddha masters, along with the pranayama training, are closely guarded secrets which are passed along by word of mouth only. Though there are various breathing exercises, it would be impossible to learn them by reading books, without knowing precisely how and what to do. The purpose of the breathing method is to maneuver life's energies, and it involves all of life's energies. Changing your mind influences these energies, and, conversely, the energies affected by changes in your breathing have an effect on the mind. It is imperative that you undertake these exercises with proper guidance, and that you learn from a teacher who is well versed in this area.

Among the various breathing exercises is one called *kumbhaka*, which involves voluntarily ceasing to breathe. The energy that flows on the right side of the body is called *pingala*, and it works to generate heat in the body. Yogis who live for decades in the bitter cold of the Himalayas are able to do so because they can control this energy well. We store food in a refrigerator to avoid it spoiling; likewise, humans can survive for a long time in the cold if they are able to control the energy on the left side of the body well. It is important to maintain the energies of both sides of the body in balance. To inhale and stop breathing is referred to as *puraka*; it awakens you inside and cleanses cells. To exhale and stop breathing is called *rechaka*; it goes deeper into the mind. To stop breathing naturally is known as *kevala kumbhaka*.

There are five types of puranas or vital energies; each one controls a specific part of the body. The five puranas are: udana, prana, samana, apana, and vyana. Samadhi Yogis can purify all functions of the mind and body, using a high-level technique called kriya. The kriya technique enables you to maintain balance, strengthen energies, shift energies in a particular direction, generate energies of fire by burning, and calm the nerves with energies of wind.

So that you can proceed with these techniques safely, the secret Himalayan teachings will guide you carefully, stage by stage. Comprehensive training is provided that will enable you to open routes to samadhi where all essences are encompassed. You will train through profound meditation and transformation will become possible; you will be reborn by powerfully shining from within. Breathing requires profound wisdom, and proper instruction is necessary, instruction that is contingent upon a particular person's level and stage. With guidance, you will be able to purify each of the pranas and cleanse the energy channels in which there are 72,000 nadis—a vast network. The techniques of *mudras* and *bandas* also purify and control these energies, cleansing all three of our bodies: the physical body, the astral body. and the causal body. By cleansing the five elements of which the human body is composed—earth, water, fire, wind, and air—the seven centers of the energy channels are purified, allowing the center of the energy's path, the *Sushumna* nadi, to open. Then you can aim toward samadhi.

Fifth step: Pratyahara (controlling the senses)

Humans are equipped with five senses—sight, hearing, smell, taste, and touch. We see with our eyes, but the eyes are not merely a sensory organ; we can also see things through the vision that rests in the back of the eyes. And, while there are five sensations for each of our sensory organs—the eyes, ears, nose, tongue, and skin—it is the mind that controls these five sensations.

Depending on our state of mind at the time, we may feel scared at seeing something, or find it beautiful or ugly, or want to see more of it, or perhaps desire to own it. In this way, when the senses are stimulated, the mind begins to function. When desires surge, the senses begin to function. Pratyahara purifies the senses and controls them. By purifying them, you can see, hear, smell, taste, and feel correctly; you can also surpass these sensations, rather than be constrained by them, and you can place yourself—your mind—in the present moment. Through strength of will, you will no longer be at the mercy of your senses.

What would happen if we threw away our attachments and saw things through the mind of *mushin* (a state of mindlessness)? When the mind is free of fixed or preconceived ideas, it is no longer reactive; it allows you to see things as they are. In other words, in order to control the senses, you must first control the mind. Then you will be able to remain un-swayed by what you see and hear; your senses will provide you with correct information, to which you will be able to give proper attention. You will make good choices. However, we humans are fond of projecting what's inside our minds onto ourselves; your past experiences will partially dictate whether you have a tendency to see things positively or negatively.

Information from the senses is immediately relayed to the mind. If the inner self is negative, you will focus on the negative, and negative words will tend to echo in your ear as a result, drawing you further into the negative and causing you to make wrong choices. In this way, feeling negative becomes something of a self-fulfilling prophecy, causing you to exert your energy in a negative direction. Because of many obsessive memories in the mind, you choose anxiety and fear. In order to avoid this, it is crucial to purify the senses and the mind. If you are aware that, "I am now choosing anxiety and fear," you ought to immediately bring yourself back to the center, to *mushin*.

To be able to do this, it is necessary to practice various exercises relating to awareness and cleansing. However, not only is it difficult to cleanse, but, generally, it is common to be swayed by the workings of the mind and the senses, simply because you don't realize you are taking things for granted. Many Indian people think of gods as infinite, pure beings blessed with wisdom; by identifying with them and the masters who have achieved a similar status—that is, by focusing their conscious minds on gods and masters—they develop and strengthen their own personas. This prevents them from being drawn like a magnet to their desires and obsessions, or from moving in capricious or negative directions at the behest of reactive mind.

I want you to learn how to control the senses and become someone who is not easily or needlessly swayed by the mind. Once you can do that, you will move in the good and right direction, thanks to your increased awareness, which will allow you to quickly distinguish between good and bad. Also, when your mind is pure and free of obsessions, you will be able to distance yourself from it without being bothered; that is, you will be able to look at it with neutrality, and eventually transcend it. By modifying your thoughts and actions in this way, you will find that you are always right where you ought to be, centered within yourself and able to survey everything that surrounds you. You will become an evolved person who is no longer pushed around for being ignorant.

Through the workshops of the Anugraha Himalayan Samadhi Program, you will become aware of each layer of the mind and remove its attachments. The Anugraha and kripa diksha courses will do much to transform you, as you receive their profound blessings. You can purify through these courses by receiving energy which allows you to feel naturally centered within yourself, without feeling anxious or irritable, or being pulled or pushed around by the senses. You must always control the senses well by knowing your mind, becoming aware of them at all times so not to be at their mercy.

Sixth step: Dharana (mental concentration technique)

Dharana is a method for mental concentration. Usually, when you are absorbed in work, it is as if you are training in mental concentration. Possessing a lot of knowledge about one's own area of work and engaging in work by concentrating creatively is a way of focusing the mind. Engaging in something we enjoy also helps to keep our minds focused; study, investigation, work, play, and hobbies are all useful forms of mental concentration. If you are working all the time, however, you run the risk of using your body and mind in an unbalanced way. It is imperative to focus through mental concentration and relax the tense mind, and, in order to rectify distortions and realign energies, it is necessary to move away from work at times. We find it difficult to concentrate when our minds are preoccupied or we are tired; it is crucial, then, to rest the mind and purify it. If you can rest more, you will be able to exert more power when it is needed. Alternatively, you can receive power by focusing your conscious mind on natural things, sacred waves, divine symbols, the supreme existence, or the enlightened masters.

The mind that is ready to accept power will do so through trust. Focus your mind on something that is pure and concentrate mentally. It is a good idea to receive this type of guidance from a master who is knowledgeable about truth. By concentrating on a pure object, the object of your concentration will empower you. In our everyday lives, while we concentrate at work and in other areas, this is usually little more than a form of consumption. By practicing the secret techniques of the Himalayan Siddha masters, you will be able to harness the mind as one and purify its energies, realigning them so that they are not consumed needlessly. This is the technique of dharana. Through it, the mind becomes truly at ease and recharged. You and your energies will become one.

Seventh step: Dhyana (becoming free)

The seventh step is *dhyana*. Through mental concentration, the flow of energy expands. You will be liberated and integrated with the energy flow—this is dhyana. In this state, you will begin to know the object of your concentration. If the mind is the object, you will come to understand it; if energy is the object, the same will happen. If you use various forms of objects, you will be able to learn about them; however, you will need to remove them if you are to advance and become the true you. With sacred objects, especially, your mind will be purified and become calm. By removing objects and transcending the mind, you return to your true self—that is, you achieve the state of enlightenment. Sensation will expand and you will know a freedom in which you are constrained by nothing, a freedom that is as deep as it is profound.

When you practice meditation, you can put your work to one side. It is fine to only meditate a little during the day. You can create a state of mindlessness in which you are not obsessed with anything by proactively cleansing the mind. Purify the mind through the high-order energy of Anugraha and use any of the various meditation techniques of the Himalayan Siddha masters to cleanse your mind and become free by removing all obsessions. While meditating, you will likely have many kinds of thoughts that recur, over and over; this is perfectly OK. These thoughts are often cues that allow you to recover details from the past and understand things whose meanings had previously been obscured. Even if these notions and thoughts come and go in your mind, it is not necessary to be controlled or swayed by them. You will gradually move beyond them and enter a deep, enlightened state of profound stillness.

The mind's activities will quieten down as you cease to consume energy, and then your energy will start to recharge. Just as a battery charges, so do the body and mind recharge, until everything is refreshed. This energy will separate from the mind and stay in your center.

Using the sound and light techniques that are passed on in the secret teachings, you can purify and cleanse your thoughts before transcending them and creating stillness. The secret teachings can make this possible surprisingly quickly.

Eighth step: To the samadhi stage finally

You will now enter the samadhi stage—that is, you are now able to attain your authentic self. There is a preceding stage of samadhi called supernatural-powered samadhi, in which you merge your consciousness with a particular object and become one with it. What we are aiming for is the final stage, the true and ultimate samadhi. This signifies that you have attained a true selfhood which can transcend your body and mind and be free. To reach this final stage is usually a long and arduous path; however, samadhi Yogis who have experienced samadhi from the secret teachings of the Himalayan Siddha masters can lead you to this path. Indeed, they show us that it is possible even for people in the twenty-first century to step onto this path.

And what's more, this can be done by only taking a little time out of your daily schedule. You will restore your natural state by controlling your mind and body and realizing who you truly are. There is divinity in nature; it has the power to produce all. You too will be able to return to creation at the true source. You acquire wisdom and power that will enable you to solve whatever problems you encounter. Your intuition and inspiration will be sharpened, and you will have the ability and power to profoundly see through all things. Through samadhi, you and your object will become one.

If the object is a material thing, then to become one with it is called *vitarka* samadhi. Once the object has been removed, it is referred to as *nirvitarka* samadhi. If the target turns into the object as the mind ponders their merging as one, it is called *vichara* samadhi, and *nirvichara* samadhi is where all is removed to reach a state of thoughtless awareness. Being integrated into a state of bliss is called *ananda* samadhi, and *amista* samadhi is being integrated into the thought of pure self. When all of these things have been removed, making you your authentic self which you can then transcend, you have attained *asampragnyata*—the ultimate samadhi. From oneness to becoming integrated with various objects, you can experience samadhi to become the true you by surpassing all of these; the samadhi to become one with the supreme being; and the ultimate samadhi, where enlightenment happens, and you transcend the self.

4. What Happens in the Process of Samadhi?

What I pray at samadhi

I received God's power by training in the Himalayas, and I was able to attain the true samadhi state and transcend death. After achieving this, I decided to help others by conducting public samadhis of the kind that were being performed by Hari Babaji and Pilot Babaji. One day, I asked Pilot Babaji to arrange a public samadhi event for me. Pilot Babaji was surprised—he thought he was the only one who could perform samadhis—but he gladly accepted my request.

I then immersed myself in samadhi and demonstrated the truth that there is great power in humans, the power to transcend death and purify the earth, to bring peace to the world and open the hearts of people. I knew that some people had paid with their lives after offering this practice; I also knew that Pilot Babaji was one of the very few people who could enable me to do this. Samadhis are risky indeed.

We become the universe by transcending death. Meditations performed in the world and yoga courses introduced to the spiritual world are merely partial, having to do with training of the physical body and strengthening of the mind through images and visual perceptions. Instructors of such courses have not transcended all in order to know samadhi as the final realm.

The same is true for Zen Buddhism, remarkable though it is; as a religion it is partial, and none of its practitioners has experienced the final realm. It is not geared toward truly experiencing meditation at its most profound level, transforming from within, eventually surpassing and becoming the true self.

Souls that are truly chosen can deepen awareness, realize the genuine truth, and walk the path. I am here to open the door to your inner soul, in order to elevate it and guide you on a journey to purify your mind, cleanse your body, and encounter your soul. I want you to become aware of the truth. I will act as the bridge that enables you to advance toward this goal, with the sole and true purpose of turning you into your authentic self. Through the secret teachings, and by experiencing numerous true samadhis, I have become thoroughly familiar with the science of the body, mind, soul, and consciousness; and I have become my true self—this is my karma. I will help you open the door to your own inner journey, so that you can be fulfilled.

The secret teachings of the Himalayan Siddha masters are now available to you through the Anugraha Himalayan Samadhi Program. Now anyone can practice and transform. By participating in the step-by-step workshops, you will practice the various secret meditation techniques and receive a high-order energy initiation. The eight steps have been updated according to the very latest bioscience; they are designed to be effective and produce quick results.

Let's meditate by tuning the channel in on me

Samadhi signifies the release of objects that cause pain on the outside, as well as attachments and obsessions that cause pain on the inside. Removing dependence on all objects other than the authentic self and those obsessions that are necessary for living, we can surpass death, become our true selves, integrate as one with divinity, and become immortal. The true self within you is called *atman*; this is the true selfhood, a shared god as the supreme existence of Brahma, the source of God's creation at the root of the cosmos. Samadhi can be traced back to the source of creative beings to reach the divinity within you; it signifies the state where you become completely immersed with the divinity of the cosmos.

To reach samadhi means becoming the true self and furthermore turning into the supreme divinity. In India, it means having attained as great a feat as any human being

All is filled with love and melts toward the divinity

could reach; to be a samadhi Yogi is to lead the most revered existence, highly regarded by people. I have performed public samadhis on numerous occasions in India; many people—from all over India—gather for them and there is always a lively, festival-like mood of celebration. You may wonder why so many people attend these events and why they get so excited. Samadhi is an ascetic training that even those who have endured severely challenging austerities cannot easily attain. As humans, we have many earthly desires that we remain unaware of. Through the never-ending cycle of reincarnation, where births and deaths are repeated throughout our past lives, we have accumulated much karma. This tarnishes the pure mind and body and exerts control over us, and the mind, being at the mercy of karma, thinks of the body and mind as the real us, and refuses to release us from pain. To encounter truth and be liberated from the body and mind may seem easy on the surface, but it is always a challenge to generate profound meditation and to further attain the samadhi state. I cannot overemphasize the fact that this is an extremely difficult feat to accomplish. In the long history of India, only a handful of people have managed to achieve this, even though many have recognized the importance of this singular feat.

Therefore, samadhi is greatly revered and respected. Priest practitioners called Sadhu, who seek truth and divinity, aim to achieve the samadhi level. Samadhi is also the ultimate goal in Yoga, and it signifies the supreme state of consciousness in all religions. By having people tune in to the channel of my samadhi through trust, I am able to harness them to my superconsciousness where peace and love spring forth. I enter into the samadhi state by offering prayers so that the people of the world can become peaceful and enjoy peace of mind. Even if you don't enter into the samadhi state yourself, your consciousness will transform by being close to someone who performs samadhi. I will be your bridge. I have samadhi with me at all times, and I share the grace as a present from the Himalayan Siddha masters, namely the gift of God's Anugraha.

Merely by being present, I enable people to transform themselves by harnessing my energy through trust. This is referred to as *darshan*—a sacred encounter. In order to ensure that this phenomenon occurs, it is recommended that you receive a high-level energy initiation or diksha, which will purify and awaken you from within. Then, after receiving this initiation, you will join with me at the level of the soul. You will be able to meditate easily as your consciousness level transforms through the touch of a Himalayan Siddha master. All you need to do is to tune in to my channel by simply trusting in samadhi. By participating in the Anugraha Himalayan Samadhi Program, you will surely transform and evolve into the best human being you can be. In doing so, and once your soul is purified, it becomes so much easier to live. The wisdom of those who have experienced samadhi is calling you to serenity and bliss. Of course, you must set the stage to prepare yourself, by deepening awareness through cleansing your body and mind.

The true path is not always smooth, but, with trust in your bridge and the necessary guidance, you can walk the path with peace of mind, even when it becomes steep and difficult to navigate; with a knowledgeable master, and the right bridge to cross, even a daunting path can become easy to walk along. All kinds of restrictions burden the mind, making it difficult to live. The purpose of profound meditation is to know death and to be aware of everything. Once you have transcended death, you will be free from pain, and the path of ignorance will be transformed into one of brightness. The Himalayan Siddha meditation is a training to create the best human being by rejuvenating the body, lightening the mind, improving the brain, and allowing the best human skills to blossom.

Samadhi to be free from illness and aging

What you need to know, as you meditate, is what is causing you pain. You must be aware that the external world, your very situation, is at the root of your pain. The path to samadhi begins when you accept that matters which become objects of attention cause pain. They appear in the form of attachments and desires that always occupy your mind, creating confusion and ignorance in your conscious mind and clouding what can be detected by the senses.

However, even accepting this is not as easy as it may seem, because such objects also bring joy to the mind, allowing you to kill time, if only for an instant, so that you feel alive for having occupied yourself temporarily through some form of superficial adornment or embellishment. This, as we know, is not a true way of living, and, furthermore, such experiences inscribe themselves in your memory as karma, further controlling and limiting your actions, and causing you to develop even more attachments. These types of attachments and mistaken notions work on a spiritual level to generate doubt. Try to think of such attachments and thoughts as demons that live within. These demons are always whispering in your ear:

"It's better not to do that; it's a waste of time. Why not enjoy yourself and have fun, rather than struggle?"

This is how the demons seduce you. Then, before you know it, you have been persuaded and you revert back to your old ways. This is because you have the desire to hold on to these unhelpful attachments, these old thoughts that have come to feel like old friends. You are afraid to let go. You worry that you will regret saying goodbye to the mind that occasioned such fun. What if the new direction you have chosen is the wrong one?

We all have things we desire: honor, status, possessions, a house, lovers, knowledge—different people desire different things. These things are karma for each of us, the accumulated results of experiences and memories from past lives. However, we seem never to realize that we are at the mercy of these desires, that these desires are, in fact, the source of our pain. Meditation can help us become aware, and once aware, we can liberate ourselves. By peeling these attachments from the mind, we can live as freely as possible, and maximize the chances of our wishes coming true.

How do our minds function? We all know that illness can be agonizing, and it is certainly true that illness can pose difficulties; however, thinking that you are sick is already a cause of pain, and what is causing the illness is actually your own karma. Most people end their lives by fighting the agony that results from karma, without realizing that other options exist. To be free from the agony of illness is not to fight the illness itself but to become aware—to realize what made you ill in the first place. It is recommended, of course, that you do what you can to improve certain habits. But why not also change your karma? If you purify it, you will change your fate, so you can be reborn successful and happy. Alas, no one knows how to do it! Not only will your pain disappear when you purify your karma, but any illness will improve right away.

The experience of samadhi makes possible all that you thought impossible. It offers answers to the biggest questions we can ask: Why do we live? What is life all about? It also answers our questions about the universe, about what the mind signifies, and who we truly are. Through samadhi, you will finally become someone who finds joy in every little thing.

Become aware of karma

In the process of walking the path toward samadhi, you will experience various occurrences as you advance your meditation.

Become aware of your own karma and change it

There is an enormous amount of karma within you, and every type of karma will sublimate as you continue to walk the path and advance to a freer realm. It is important to know that this process can, at times, make you feel quite miserable. This is simply a result of karma that has accumulated over the course of your life being released. Try not to feel anxious—be grateful that you have been given this opportunity to know the existence of your karma, accept it for what it is, and forge ahead with humility.

Karma can explode at times—what was inherently, silently there gushes out. Sometimes the wound is not as clean as it might be, and there is a risk of infection. You must get rid of it all, though, even if it feels painful at the time. But rest assured: the way to neutralize the risk of infection is to trust the guru who is showing you the way, and to fully believe that you are walking on the right path. This belief will ease your pain.

The most important thing is to *believe*—to believe that you are made to be alive through the divine power. If you doubt this, your risk of infection will increase, but if you believe, you will be securely protected by the divine power, and able to become a more resilient and kinder person by showing gratitude as you remain humble. Through it all, you will be more open to accept the divine power. And you will be able to smoothly purify your karma. Droplets of honeydew bestowed by the divinity will accumulate within you. However, if you remain headstrong and distrustful of others, no energy will flow toward you. No honeydew droplets will accumulate.

You may think it is good to strive and work hard; I used to strive too, in order to live a clean and honest life. However, this type of striving can result in pushing good things away; so that the emotions harden, and you end up striving even more. I used to think, "I'm trying so hard to live my life correctly, but something doesn't feel right, it feels forced, and I'm certainly not enjoying myself." Eventually

I realized that everything was due to my ego, and I began to shift my thoughts to something more along the lines of, "I want to do away with pain by removing it and releasing it completely." In other words, unless you have the strong desire to let go of yourself, you will not be able to walk this path. If you can't let go, your mind will soon be caught up in the swirl of information and the surfeit of "stuff," and you be overwhelmed again.

Our lives are determined by the karma we possess. Many of us are destined to remain ignorant, never to become aware. However, it is natural for people to evolve. To be awakened and to know the truth is to live genuinely. This is the best life and the surest means of human evolution. This is indeed the path to samadhi, and in order to walk this path, you must proceed by trusting and being humble, getting rid of desires, and banishing the doubting mind. My samadhi exists in order for you to live the very best life.

Become free of illness

The path to samadhi is the path to absolute happiness and enlightenment. Yoga is generally known as a way to maintain health and is usually thought of as consisting of physical exercises. Someone might practice yoga to improve their chances of staying healthy, or because it makes them feel more at ease. We might describe it as a temporary release from pain.

When one is diagnosed with an illness, it causes distress as well as pain. The thought of having an illness creates anxiety, and the mind starts to think that the illness might never improve—we worry we may never be cured. We fight the illness by going to various doctors and hospitals, getting injections, and receiving one prescription after another. However, no peace comes our way, as long as there is anxiety. Is it satisfying to visit a doctor and be told that you have this or that disease, and to leave with medication for treating it?

Does it help to have a label affixed to your illness? I don't think so. Merely to be told that we have a certain illness only magnifies our anxiety. And anxiety in turn breeds more pain.

It is so much better, then, to try to realize that illness can be a fortunate signal, a warning that something inside us is askew, and needs our attention. Often the reason is that our lives are in disarray, our minds confused, our eating habits awry, etc. As you practice meditation and begin to walk the path, the karma that has made you sick will burn off, and you will gradually—and quite naturally—free yourself of the disease.

Here, in these pages, is the chance to encounter true Yoga, the Himalayan Siddha Yoga, as the path to the truth. It is the path to happiness where you become a complete human being by understanding everything while maintaining balance. The true Yoga provides graces from the ultimate samadhi wisdom and generates healing at the root. It is a true health management method for genuine healing, purifying and developing the mind, cleansing the body from deep within, maintaining balance, and producing profound meditation. Rid yourself of all attachments and become enlightened—complete freedom can be yours on the path to samadhi!

YAWN MEDITATION

When you have been sitting in the same position, working hard for many hours, force out a yawn as if you had suddenly become an animal. This simple meditation method helps restore you to your natural self. (Please be careful to choose an appropriate time and place to practice this meditation, so you don't annoy those around you.)

CHAPTER FOUR

Aim for a True Way of Living

1. Learn the Workings of the Mind

Yoga makes you an upbeat person

It is important to align yourself physically if you are to successfully practice mental concentration. In doing so, you can maintain the balance of energy so as to anchor the mind, which might otherwise go all over the place, instead of converging as one. Yoga privileges the form in which no worldly thoughts are allowed to enter. There is a sitting pose that induces stability in order to practice meditation. The spine is straightened, up and down, and the shoulders are positioned horizontally; when the tip of your nose and your navel are aligned, you can sit easily as your energy is stabilized. This pose allows the mind to feel at ease, too. In this way, the body and mind work together, mutually supporting each other. It often happens that, when the body doesn't feel right, it causes the mind to feel depressed (and vice versa); but, when the body is correctly aligned, the mind brightens again. This is not the same as having the body temporarily assume a healthy state as a result of the mind having satisfied one of its desires. There are those, of course, who continue to pretend to be upbeat by forcing themselves; all this does, however, is indicate a lack of awareness.

In India, those who are devout sometimes perform what we might call channeling: they assume different characters and utter words from their subconscious mind. Even though it may be temporary, they believe themselves to be taken over by characters other than themselves, and when they return to their normal selves, they are completely exhausted. This is due to eating away at the physical body by disrupting the balance of the mind, which becomes too strong. You cannot acquire peace of mind unless you become your true self by purifying yourself of the internal energies of these attachments. Body and mind are continuously impacting each other, and it is crucial to maintain the two in balance.

However, the mind has its proclivities, and it is highly challenging to change them. It is especially difficult to see into your own mind and assess it correctly. Despite this, we like to think that we have little difficulty in seeing into others' minds. We may be able to do so, if only superficially, but the fact remains that we seem never to know our own minds. Sometimes we even have trouble in correctly identifying whether we are feeling positive or negative, upbeat or somber.

Someone who was brought up in a quiet home may prefer a quiet environment and feel uncomfortable in a place that is loud and bright. On the other hand, someone who grew up in a bustling, active home may feel uncomfortable in a very quiet place. However, we know better than to say that quiet equals dark, and that noisy equals cheerful, not to mention the fact that there are infinite shades of light and dark. Also, suppressed energy can turn you into a heavy, somber person. But when you meditate and practice Himalayan Siddha Yoga, you will clean your energies and maintain balance from deep within. When you are fully relaxed and at ease you will naturally become an upbeat, lighthearted person. As long as you continue to practice the secret Himalayan Siddha meditation, you will be able to alternate between quiet and lively with ease. In other words, all of your inherent skills will open up. You will find satisfaction in being quiet but at the same time you will access a different type of positive energy that may well cause you, as the saying goes, to jump for joy. You will be filled with life's energy and your mind will expand to its full breadth.

Attachments are the same as heavy baggage

As we discussed earlier, the mind and body are closely inter-twined and always influence each other; when the body is not feeling well, it is inevitable for the mind to feel low. In order to prevent the mind from turning somber, all you have to do is not let your mind be impacted by your body. When the mind gets somber, it turns its switch to negativity; what you must do is somehow switch it to positivity. Try to become someone who is free and not constrained by anything. By this I mean that it is necessary to become someone who is not overwhelmed by their environment, someone who can accept everything with gratitude and not be obsessed.

It is no good to feel depressed simply because it is rain-ing, or to feel out of sorts because you don't have much money. Also, it is not enough to feel upbeat if you are out having fun with your friends, but, as soon as you get home, you feel lonely and depressed. That your mind is working in this way is proof that you are living by over-ly relying on something external all the time. When you are easily swayed by the opinions or knowledge of others, your mind will always be confused. It is crucial, therefore, to actually realize, feel, and experience, to be aware and to really know, deeply. In order to develop awareness, your karma necessarily comes into play. Illnesses are necessary, and so are failures and disappointments, along with every-thing else you have experienced so far.

You will release all of your stagnant energies one by one, through the blessings of Anugraha. You will let go of neg-ative events by understanding them, and positive events will no longer obsess you. This is because you have begun to walk on the path that leads to enlightenment. Negative mind can be dissolved through daily samadhi meditation, various Himalayan Siddha meditation techniques, a kripa course, and special secret techniques, as well as both basic and advanced courses and training camps.

If you are already practicing a certain program that causes your energy level to be invigorated, you may feel the power to be a little on the weak side. This may be due to unconsciously excluding the very acts of accepting and understanding. Or, your karma may be light, and so you actually may not be able to feel that you are changing. If your karma is heavy, you will experience actually the priceless feeling of letting your various attachments go. You may well exclaim to yourself, with some astonishment, "It's amazing that I can actually feel this light and free!" It must feel like this when you get rid of pain. It is like the feeling of finally being able to put down a heavy piece of baggage—it is as though a big burden has been lifted off your shoulders after much time has been spent enduring it and complaining about how heavy it was.

The mind worries and gets anxious with little provocation; we are often wondering if we are OK or not. And, when it feels as though there is no way out, we can sometimes feel as if we want to die. Despite the fact that we realize the pain was nothing as soon as it is gone, we feel the pain acutely as long as we are embroiled in it. Yes, it will diminish with the passage of time, and yes, it will feel like nothing one day, but these types of karma are habitual, and repeat themselves again and again. This is because we hold the cause within ourselves.

To a greater or lesser extent, we are obsessed with external things and hold certain prejudiced notions. We tend to forget that our obsessions themselves cause pain, wreaking havoc on our lives by causing our minds to become hard and inflexible. Clearly, the thing to do is to change this state of mind: assume a state of mindlessness and take pleasure in everything through a combination of delight and innocent glee. Out of this, something fresh in you will definitely begin to grow. To take a mundane example: you may put off a particular task, thinking it couldn't possibly be something you would like to do, only to find that it is unexpectedly easy—and not only that, but fun—once you actually knuckle down to do it.

Jesus Christ, Buddha, and great saints throughout history have preached in favor of and attested to the greatness of freedom. Jesus said that we are love, beings born to know the truth. I wonder if this is true. Buddha said, "We are beings with wisdom." I wonder if this is true. And he added, "We are pure, free beings without pain." I really wonder if this is true! If what the saints have said is really true, is it OK to end one's life? Life gets more complicated if you think of it as challenging; you have nothing to lose to begin with. We are born naked and we die naked, and we have to leave everything behind that we have accumulated on this earth. Your energies shift to different locations when you employ this way of thinking, and possibilities open up.

You must purify the karma that exerts a negative pull on your body. You can do this by allowing yourself to be guided—to a stillness that is profound—by the secret Himalayan Siddha training techniques.

Profound decisions make wishes come true

Your mind gets overwhelmed when you are under stress; it starts to whirl in overdrive, and you feel exhausted as a result. If this continues, you feel tired before you have even done anything.

We all have too many things on our minds, and this causes us to worry about what would happen if we lost one or all of them. This anxiety can easily turn into fear. Why not simply learn to meditate, in pursuit of the truth? Perhaps because we have a mental image of meditation as simply sitting, and, because we are not familiar with its effects, it strikes us as merely a waste of valuable time.

You will eventually encounter your true self

What in the world can we lose, however, by learning to meditate to seek the truth? Is it really a waste of time? Are you really too busy? Yes, you need the guidance of a master who is knowledgeable about the truth, but, under this guidance, you will soon find that you have more time rather than not enough, simply because, with your energies usefully aligned, your body will no longer require as much sleep. Also, you will no longer crave such elaborate meals, and your food budget will decrease, and so you will find yourself, not only with more time, but also more money. You will no longer feel as though you have to reach for this or that book, forcing yourself to learn more and panicking about not reading more books and magazines. You will already have become aware of many things. Your intuition will be sharpened, and your creativity will refuse to lie dormant. Gradually, you will begin to feel joy while simply walking or relaxing at home. And, instead of only feeling fulfilled when you are praised in front of others or when you receive something valuable, you will feel happy when you get rid of something or when you give something to others. You will begin to know how to turn every instant into a joyous experience.

The mind is indeed fickle. Even if you decide something today, you may be vacillating over it tomorrow. It can often be difficult to make decisions. The strong, pure willpower called sankalpah can help with this; it can help you become what you want and realize what you wish. However, in order to reach it, your mind needs to be thoroughly clean, and you must be in the habit of using it for good causes, because, when the mind is clean and functioning well, what you wish for can actually come true. No matter what the circumstances may be or whatever you do, you must never use the mind in a bad way to hurt others or to satisfy your own desires. It is possible to make someone ill by holding a grudge against them; therefore, those who train and meditate must rid themselves of desires and use their power for good deeds only.

Our minds and bodies are precious gifts that are temporarily bestowed onto us by God. Because of this, we have the responsibility to pass our DNA—namely samskara, information from past lives—to those who will be born next. We are responsible for honing it, and for looking after it. If we passed it to the next person without polishing it, our soul would be reborn in its tainted condition, as is, and the next person would suffer the consequences. In other words, we would be held responsible, even after death. We must take care, therefore, and clean our soul to ensure its good condition for being reborn—a good service for the person who will inherit it. This is also crucial for our own journey after death.

Someone once asked me, "Isn't the act of refining yourself a selfish one?" No, not at all. Yes, we know people who develop their skills in order to win over others, to obtain a good employment opportunity, or make better friends, but encountering the truth and refining one's self have nothing to do with such competitive behavior. The purpose is always to surpass fear, release everything, and purify—that is, to become a peaceful person filled with love and wisdom. It means to share peace and love with those around you. And it also means to provide hope. Once your mind has been cleaned and your wave motion purified, your immediate family members will also be purified, and the spirits of your ancestors will be purged. This will impact those around you; indeed, you will heal those around you with love, and make them happy. As the reverberations spread out, the dream of a world at peace starts to seem less fanciful.

The core of training is to be grateful

As you proceed with the sacred techniques of the Himalayan Siddha Yoga training, your head will clear as areas that are not even visible are purified. This is something that modern medicine is unable to fathom. There is no great difference, for example, between the brains of those who are considered smart and those who are not. As people accumulate various types of experiences, the experiences are stored in their bodies and minds as memories in their DNA. These are not limited to happy experiences, of course, but include painful, sad, and difficult experiences as well. These can be purified through meditation. As your past lives are reflected and resurface in the process of training, you may feel your blood freeze as you are exposed to a pandemonium of past experiences.

Perhaps you were bullied in the past and you patched over this memory by holding a grudge; when you meditate, the original experience may appear before your eyes, perhaps in a quite dramatic form. Please remember that it is possible for your meditation to turn in an unpleasant, perhaps even nasty, direction, even when you believe you are sitting and practicing correctly.

There is definitely a right frame of mind fro practicing; its core consists of gratitude. This may sound vague, but I assure you it is possible to put into actual practice, by not taking another's life, not acting violently, not being critical of others, etc. Also, by transforming the act of not robbing or stealing into a more proactive one, you can practice the act of giving to others. Using the various detailed techniques of the secret teachings, along with the guidance of how to regulate your external actions without using energy negatively, you will be using your mind in the best way possible in daily life.

Training to show gratitude in all things

The central, most important thing is to trust the master who shows you the path, and to follow them. There are many yoga and spiritual instructors, just as there are many different training techniques, but it is rare indeed to encounter a Himalayan master who knows the ultimate truth. It is imperative to be guided by such a master if you are to employ the techniques of the secret teachings correctly and enter into a profound state. As with anything—sports, for example—it is important to start with the basics and to proceed by being taught by a teacher who is versed in the field. In doing so, you will feel secure, which in turn will have a beneficial effect on the pace at which you learn. Peace of mind cannot be overestimated.

Become free by having karma purified

Peace of mind is something we all seek in our lives. You may get a momentary thrill out of groping your way along in the dark, but danger is by your side at all times, preventing you from feeling truly at ease, and slowing your progress toward your goals. The secret Himalayan teachings are the path to truth, on which you can evolve yourself to the ultimate by receiving the blessings of the world; at the same time, the path leads you to a life of giving blessings to those around you. On this path, it is particularly important to be able to feel at ease—indeed, you can only proceed freely and easily on this path when you have peace of mind.

In practicing meditation, it is natural to wonder if you are "doing it" correctly, but you are safe as long as you enjoy the protection of a master. Through meditation, your karma will be cleansed, and you will gradually start to experience life as joyful rather than painful. Indeed, you will come to appreciate life from the bottom of your heart. Through being introduced to a master who is well versed in truth, you will be able to learn quickly and safely, without feeling any fear at all. I truly envy you for being presented with this wonderful opportunity; through the secret teachings, you will swiftly access the path it took me decades to attain. What took me forty years to learn has, in essence, been packaged and wrapped up for you, and is now, in the form of the secret teachings, presented to you as a gift.

Meditation can be practiced no matter where you are—please don't feel that you need to set aside a special room or place. It can be any corner of any room; indeed, it is precisely by meditating that the corner becomes the sacred space. You begin by calming your mind for a short time each day and taking a first look into your inner self. This is all you need to do; however, it is under the premise of being guided, gently but correctly. Gradually, you will enter deeper by merging your mind, body, and thoughts as one. Then you will begin to experience various thoughts surging within, and you can let them go, one by one.

However, there may be many occasions at the beginning when you find it difficult to meditate. This is because it is not so easy to concentrate mentally. First, you must begin by sitting; this will remove barriers of the mind and allow the body to be free. Many experiences from past lives as well as your current one are etched in the mind and body as memories, and it is necessary that you remove them as you move through the process of cleansing the mind and body.

Sometimes you will find it difficult to get rid of the barriers of the mind by yourself. Various techniques that are made available through the secret teachings can help with this. For example, aside from moving various parts of the body, there are methods that use sound to release various experiences from the mind. The Anugraha Himalayan Samadhi Program includes various workshops and meditation exercises for removing barriers from the mind. By putting these exercises into practice, you will purify your mind and body and improve your powers of mental concentration. And, eventually, you will encounter your true self.

2. What It Means to Truly "Live"

No happiness comes unless the inner environment is aligned

It is possible to lose, in an instant, the precious existence you thought would last forever. It is crucial, therefore, to always think what you ought to believe in your life. How would you spend the time you had left, for example, if you found out that tomorrow was to be your last day on earth? We all live with the assumption that there is always a tomorrow. Because of it, we spend much of our time complaining about this and that—we simply can't help ourselves. However, if you realized you had today and tomorrow *only*, every moment would suddenly become precious. You would remember, with fondness, every one of the people you ever cared about. You would forget all the things you had been frustrated with, all the things you felt resentful toward. You would feel forgiveness toward everything and everyone. Your desires and obsessions would rapidly dissipate. You may have wanted this or that, or have been hoping a particular situation would occur, but now you realize that things of this kind can no longer be helped. At this point in your life, it is no longer useful to fight.

Wouldn't you, logically, begin to think about how to spend the limited time you had left in the best way you possibly could? This is how people feel when they are exposed to the vast wilderness of the Himalayas. There is nothing there—no housing, no food, no clothes. Although the temperature is below freezing, there is no heating equipment whatsoever. There is no comfort to be had, at all. Those who train there live in the caves. In such an environment, there is nothing to lose. When you have removed yourself from your family and society, all you have left, as resources, are your body and mind. Your body and mind are your only tools for registering experience. Therefore, it is only safe to train in the Himalayas when your mind and body are sound and when the bulk of your attachments have been safely removed from your mind.

We feel cold and heat through our physical body. Since there is no heating of any kind in the Himalayas, you have to overcome the low temperatures with your body. In other words, in the Himalayas, the body and mind have to function as an alternative to a heater. The Himalayas would be a terrible environment in which to succumb to illness, or for your mind to be inundated with distracting thoughts. But it is possible to live a relaxed, comfortable life there, provided your physical body is healthy and your mind is at peace. We find it hard to think this way; we like to complain, and we don't feel well, and we always look for what might be amiss, even when our needs appear to be well met. This, again, is one of our minds' proclivities. You are destined to repeat the same patterns unless you practice being grateful in everything. One of the purposes of your training is to modify the conscious mind. Unless your inner self is changed, you will not acquire true happiness or peace of mind.

Trust without judging

We are all connected with the divinity at the profound level. And I am conveying blessings of the sacred Himalayan Siddha teachings to you, assuming the role of bridge. I want to offer you the graces of the Himalayan Siddhas, without causing you to leave your current situation and circumstances behind. What I want to convey to you the most is that, through the secret teachings, you will be securely tied to the divinity and able to purify your inner being at the fastest speed, thereby awakening the sacredness within you, restoring brightness, filling with joy, love, peace, and freedom, and able to live a beautiful life.

By the way, what does it mean to truly live life? I imagine you were brought up by parents who always told you not to do this or that, and that you were encouraged to adhere to certain moralistic rules. I don't doubt, of course, that your parents wanted you to thrive, to always be safe, and to lead a respectable life. However, it is possible for good advice and good morals to backfire—for example, when you have been told the same thing one thousand times, to the extent that you feel sick and tired and only hear the words as a kind of irritating noise. And I am sure we have all encountered those "good kids" who listen and obey their parents, but who strike us as somehow too stiff and not as fun-loving as children ought to be. Even if the words are coming from parents who care about their children, unless the children themselves are allowed to have experiences, the words won't reach their souls or be particularly effective. This, then, is the lesson: in order to transform, you must realize yourself.

Also, it is crucial that you continue to exert effort unflaggingly, and that you truly want the transformation to occur. There will be no growth if you go along as before, satisfying your egotistical desires and living selfishly. There may be situations where you feel distressed and find it difficult to continue, or where you struggle to stay centered in yourself, and to maintain the correct balance; however, that is due to your ego resisting, and, in order not to succumb to it, you must maintain a high level of willpower. If you don't, you will undoubtedly suffer setbacks.

The mind is crafty and will unconsciously move in the direction of comfort and ease to prevent further effort, or in the direction of what you were used to before as habit. You must realize that this is not the direction in which you will really grow. The mind is merely being calculating in its subtle way, finding easy avenues of escape so as not to hurt the ego. This is an instinctive mechanism of self-defense which we all have. It is little wonder, then, that human relationships often don't work smoothly, as humans—with their self-defense mechanisms fully intact—interact with each other in society. Mistrustful, insecure individuals who interact with each other tend only to breed more mistrust and insecurity as a result.

I sometimes feel that there has been no time in history when human relationships have been as shallow as they are now. I want you to find your true self by getting rid of your prejudiced mind, removing all mistrust and insecurity, and nurturing trust and love. In the process of encountering your true self, you will be able to interact with others with understanding and respect, while at the same time accepting and loving yourself.

All of us, of course, need to learn such basic rules of social life as good manners, but we need to be aware of the danger—namely, that we can lose sight of our very essence if we allow ourselves to be overly bound by formalities. You will be able to reconnect with your essence naturally by receiving blessings of good energy through your encounters with a master. These blessings will significantly augment and develop your trusting mind.

Know what's most important for you

When Buddha acquired enlightenment in India many hundreds of years ago, there were numerous philosophical schools being established which were restricted to various styles. Ceremonies were held in which live animals were sacrificed as offerings, to improve the chances of prayers being answered by the multitudinous gods. Seeing this, Buddha began to preach that there was no true liberation unless one became aware through meditation, and that it was important to be aware of one's own self. Meditation is discussed in the Vedas (the oldest religious scriptures); Buddha preached about the truth by bringing it down to

No stepping forward until the present is accepted

a level that people could easily understand. And he be-seeched everyone to renounce the world.

Although today's young people may not realize it, the advanced nations of the world have become glutted with abundance, with every convenience you could imagine, in recent decades. When I reflect back on my days as a child, I could hardly have imagined, then, that we would see an era so rich in material wealth. In the days of my childhood, in the postwar era, we suffered privation due to many provisions being in short supply. Today we live in a blessed era where anything and everything can be easily obtained. However, while we are blessed to live in such an enriched society, many of us feel far from satisfied. What seemed satisfying yesterday no longer piques our interest today. We feel that something has to be wrong, if we are not happier today than we were yesterday; this has be-come our obsession.

We will never be satisfied, however, as long as we contin-ue to seek happiness in material goods. Acquiring things in this way always leads only to momentary fulfilment, to fleeting happiness, at the very best. We always think we ought to be richer and happier. Even if we find love, we immediately worry we will lose it. In fact, we make ourselves feel anxious and insecure, because if we don't, we worry that we are not feeling as anxious as we ought to, and we agonize over what could possibly be wrong. We will never make progress this way. What is important is to develop and maintain a state of happiness, and this is done by realizing what is most important to you.

One day, once of my students said to me, "I am always feeling anxious. I realize this state of being is no good, but I continue to suffer every day, not knowing how to get rid of this anxiety." I answered thus: "Please try to envision that you are closely tied to the divinity and that it is in the center of your being at all times. If you can't envision this, please connect with the sacred Himalayan teachings first. By receiving high-order graces from a master, you will transform your inner self and become happy. You will be linked to an eternal existence, peace of mind, and power. Your anxiety will disappear if you harness yourself to the eternal existence, which is also your true self. Distance yourself from your mind; try to develop new and correct habits. Your anxiety appears to come from your past experiences, which can be released through samadhi meditation. And by firmly believing that you can definitely change, you will be able to set your mind at ease. And furthermore, by asking who you are, you can proceed to advance your consciousness."

How to make good energy flow

We live because we receive power from infinite beings, and this power makes our minds and bodies function. The circuit that is supposed to flow smoothly, however, is disrupted here and there, causing us to lose our balance as the mind and body become clouded with little or no awareness of who we really are. This causes blockages which in turn disrupt the flow of our energies, so that we are no longer able to effectively and correctly use them. It is crucial to fix this circuit by discovering the areas that are out of shape and damaged.

You have your car inspected from time to time, making necessary adjustments and replacing defective parts. If parts are malfunctioning without being noticed or fixed, you can find yourself in danger. So, too, if parts of us are malfunctioning, we run the risk of there being serious consequences. I refer, of course, to karma from past lives; knowledge of this karma is what we have been referring to as awareness and is essential if you are to proceed along the path to awakening.

Through the practical Himalayan teachings, such as awareness meditation, Siddha kriya exercises, and mantras, you can burn off and purify karma. The secret teachings allow you to repair or replace parts as needed, perform specific adjustments, and confirm that your overall wiring is correct. The rest is up to you and will depend on the extent to which you trust in existence at the source, and allow your good energies to flow. Through these energies, your fate will improve, your doubts and anxieties will melt away, and your body and mind will heal. Your wisdom will spring forth and you will begin to see your true self. Once you reach this stage, you can think about how to deploy your wonderful assets. This will link with and determine how blissful you become. Once you are connected to your master through trust, transformation will quickly take place; blessings will be generated as your master acts as a bridge, integrating you with existence at the source.

I mentioned earlier that all of us are connected to the divinity at the profound level, and that I am merely serving as a linking connection or bridge. Through the union between you and me, you will be strengthened as you are tied to the divinity. As a result, you will acquire unbeatable power, wisdom, and love. As a Himalayan Siddha master, I can offer all of this to you as a gift.

The notion of knowledge as panacea is mistaken

Meditation is a boom industry these days. I believe people are drawn to meditation because their lives are so busy. When people are so wrapped up in work, so bewildered by human relationships, it is only natural for them to seek solace and peace of mind. We put time and effort into sorting out one problem after another, as we try to restore our own selves. This can be partially effective, of course, but the problem with resorting to all-purpose techniques is that they tend not to solve problems at the root. Temporary respite is OK, as far as it goes, but a setback usually follows soon after.

You will acquire indomitable power, wisdom, and love

For example, let's assume that you are the manager of a corporation, and you are attempting to reassign responsibilities and relocate positions among your staff; however, when you attempt to assess strength of character by forcibly testing the patience of certain staff members, the situation starts to deteriorate. What is important above all else in human relationships is trust. Great love and trust alone will melt everything by swallowing all available problems whole. And you will be able to cultivate this type of great love within you through the meditation techniques of the secret teachings. To think that you can solve everything through knowledge alone is vanity. You may know success in specific areas, but you will never come close to comprehending the whole.

There are specialists with the necessary skills in all particularized areas of study, conducting research in their areas of expertise. Much progress is made as a result. And yet, are we really doing much more than scratching the surface? Yes, we enrich our stores of knowledge in certain areas, but what about the overall balance?

If you become a person who can view everything in its entirety, you can live without wandering aimlessly, without feeling hectic and claustrophobic. Realistically speaking, as we know, no one is perfect, and rare indeed is the person who is able to view the entirety while remaining free of any issues of their own. For ninety-nine percent of people, we may say that they try to get a little creative with some method or other, or with some pseudo-technique, but they will eventually either give up after having realized its limitations, hit a wall through exhaustion, or completely deplete their vital force. To transform into a person who can view the entirety, we need to remove the ego. This can be done by making meditation part of your daily routine.

Human values are not determined by work alone

If you work in business, the chances are that you are under stress. Plus, mental concentration leads to exhaustion. You need to relax, but how can you, focused as you are on the bottom line? What do you think we need in this day and age when we are inundated with material goods? When supplies are needed in society and a company is experiencing a period of growth, outcomes are readily verified. But the time to test corporate durability is when the growth period has ended, and saturation has set in. Then, it becomes a daunting task to further expand the company's operations, or even to maintain them. For this reason, corporate managers are working extremely long hours, in an intensely competitive environment.

When you work for a company, it is easy to ignore the fact that your body and mind are under stress. We hear the terrible stories of people who have been driven to commit suicide as they are worn out, physically and mentally, and simply unable to rehabilitate themselves in society. It is indeed true that the mind can be broken, just the same as the body. Despite this fact, many people continue to work in the corporate world.

The corporations, of course, have to maintain some sort of balance if their employees are to be able to function; otherwise energies will deplete until the employees burn out. Workers are not disposable; their energies must be developed. It is crucial, however, that these people don't merely learn skills for work but also maintain the circuits in which power at the source is bestowed.

This is not limited to corporations. In the male-dominated society of Japan, it is thought to be especially rewarding to be always engrossed in your work, and to work tirelessly in the interest of increasing the bottom line. Men who do so are treated with great respect. It is certainly quite appealing to see people working hard in society, and their efforts are admirable. However, human values cannot be measured by work alone. Are we content to assign no value to our other attributes? If you aim to be complete as a human being, you can incorporate the meditation techniques of the Himalayan Siddha masters into your daily routine. Why not be reborn as a new leader for a new era? Shed your stresses, overflow with vital energy, and be empowered with wisdom and kindness. Then you will truly find living life to be invigorating.

3. Seize and Surpass the Changes

Stir things up with normal changes in abnormal areas

When everything is a matter of habit, you can continue in the same groove without much effort; however, accumulated tension can still wear you down. It is always crucial to maintain, and sustain, effort and willpower. Moreover, you cannot just choose whatever you like when it comes to making a living, and you should try to avoid letting the little chores pile up, even if you hate doing them.

When you do get to finally relax at home on your days off, you may feel some stress at the thought of having to return to work. We often choose to remedy our situation by opting for a new and different environment; but, no sooner have we started to take it for granted than we begin to lose sight of its blessings. A healthy person will never notice how fortunate they are to be enjoying every meal. And if you are ill, you can attempt to maintain balance by taking medication for the part of the body which is affected, but it is often the case that other parts of the body are negatively affected by this same medication. We tend to overlook this, simply because we are not aware, and we usually make our discovery too late. A practice of daily meditation will help you avoid this. It will relax your mind and body and untangle any hardened or negative areas.

No transformation unless you change

It is very common for needless thoughts, futility, or imbalance to accumulate in our lives and dispositions. It is crucial to allow good changes to take place, if normalcy is to be restored. We tend to want to maintain the status quo, if only inadvertently; it feels safe to avoid change and remain the same. We usually assume, subconsciously or otherwise, that change is negative; by nature, we are resistant to it. The prospect makes us anxious, and we are afraid we will somehow lose something in the process. We need to realize when change is not only appropriate but also a plus.

In the past, we tended to rely on the myth of security, which was based on the notion that we would always be safe. Perhaps we believed that the company we worked for would never go under, or that our family would never be visited by illness. Even if we saw that the economy was starting to fray around the edges, we nevertheless believed that our assets were secure. However, there is no evidence whatsoever to support these notions, and, in recent times, the myth of security has definitively crumbled. It should be evident to all that we are mired in insecurity.

Even so, there are some who only see the surface and who remain quite satisfied, getting along in society, more or less, having a reasonably stable home life, enjoying hobbies, etc. Under these circumstances, however, the physical body is definitely changing. The change may be subtle at first and entirely unnoticeable, but it will advance, until one day there is a real risk of succumbing, of having a breakdown and feeling entirely out of sorts. Once such a thing happens, it is impossible not to worry. Fear, anxiety, and medical examinations will follow. What was believed in for so long has been disrupted.

Sadly, it is often too late when this finally happens. But if we had been able to notice subtle changes at the beginning, and had then taken action swiftly, the problem may not have become so serious. Please don't be afraid to change. Change is essentially good because it allows you to become aware of abnormalities and to realize what is genuine.

It may seem obvious to say so, but you will not change unless you implement a change, or, perhaps, multiple changes. You must realize that you yourself will only change when you accept these changes. You will begin to become aware by realizing, "Aha! What is this? It feels different than before." If you remain suspicious of change because you are completely immersed in your current situation, no changes will occur, and your chance of realization will be lost. Realization is essential if you are to make the necessary modifications to restore yourself to a normal, stable condition. This does not mean, however, that the work is done once balance has been restored. After making the changes that were needed, you will soon get used to your new condition, and, before you know it, you will once more sooner stay put than make any further modifications that might be required.

What is essential, then, is to reexamine yourself from a vantage of awareness. You can reflect back on your life up to now: how you have chosen to live, what problems have arisen, etc. Explore who you truly are. This is the work of understanding yourself, your temperament, habits, and character traits. Consider your ability to change as proof of being alive and believe that you have what it takes to make progress. It is crucial to maintain balance by making the necessary changes.

Changes occur due to imbalance

Changes don't occur when there is balance. Changes occur because of being imbalanced. Water flows from high to low due to an imbalance caused by gaps on earth.

Without these gaps, water would stay where it was. When water changes position, it flows, and to flow is to be alive. This does not mean that we should allow dirty water to flow indiscriminately. By letting clean water flow in a good direction, new life emerges, and plants and animals flourish. We can direct our own energies in the same way.

The bigger the gaps, the more accelerated the flow becomes. This allows changes to occur more rapidly. This force is nature's way of maintaining balance and is referred to as natural recovery action or natural healing ability. It is the ability to restore an original state by maintaining balance, as when cells vigorously activate. As we age, however, imbalance tends to manifest in the form of blockage, and changes rarely occur. Our cells function more slowly, and lethargy sets in. It is crucial, therefore, to maintain the balance with the support of purification and empowerment; this way, you will be able to restore yourself to your original natural state without any deviations.

The key here is to focus on the change itself. It is not a shift in a different, unstable direction; there is no need for anxiety or fear. If change itself should somehow cause additional problems, you will be able to handle them calmly—indeed, you may even derive pleasure from the process of changing. Examine yourself closely and look to see where you are headed. This too is part of awareness.

If you have no power, however, or if there is no trust in your heart, or your mind attaches itself to fear, you will find the process of change to be arduous and difficult. If you lack faith and trust, you will struggle to see matters correctly—that is, with mindlessness. As we have discussed, the mind is prone to attachment and movement; it is no easy matter to persuade the mind not to function. It has its proclivities as well as its memories. Rather than resisting its workings, try to consciously and intentionally tap into good things.

Changes to the physical body are linked to rebirth

If you feel in a great deal of pain, it is because you are not ready to accept that everything is going to change. *Everything* in this context includes yourself and others, as well as external phenomena. In order to feel no pain or lessen your pain as much as possible, it is advisable to try to view matters by pulling away from them, if you can.

Your heart aches if you feel that those who are close to you are giving you the cold shoulder. But you can learn from this by treating it as an opportunity to examine yourself. Perhaps you have been expecting too much of others? After all, people don't exist in order to make others feel good about themselves. Normally, we are all desperately trying to protect ourselves. This can be quite visible at times: when people are doing their own thing, and that thing is something they enjoy, they can appear quite cold to others.

We try to be nice to others because it makes us feel better about ourselves; it may not necessarily be the case that we have been thinking about the other person that much. Sometimes we act generously out of self-defense; sometimes we feel envious when we see how nice people can be to others. Or, again, we may begin to rely on the kind gestures of others and assume that the niceties we have come to expect from them will last forever.

To put this another way, we feel pained because we tend to judge others through our own self-serving interpretations and assumptions, and we are overly swayed by the words and actions of others. We struggle, compare, and judge. We look in from the outside, weighing the pros and cons, becoming even more demanding if we feel we are not getting what we want. Through ignorance, we maintain balance by blaming others and affirming ourselves, but this cannot be sustained indefinitely. In other words, everything goes up and down, and goes up and down over and over again, in order to maintain balance.

Living creatures live and die; markets rise and fall. Everything goes through changes. It is imperative that you firmly grasp this notion. The pure, straightforward attitudes of youth change as we grow; notions attach to our minds and harden, becoming tainted as we overly rely on them. Nostalgia is usually the result: "Ah, things were better in the old days." This, too, is simply another attachment.

There are those who are reluctant to reflect on the past, and who refuse to accept it, as it only holds bad memories. However, unless such people undertake to make changes for themselves, they will end up repeating precisely the same patterns as before. Present misfortune will not cease, unless it is forced to through the process of cleansing. Without realizing this and without accepting the past, the future can only be negative.

We judge events and experiences against a yardstick that we cling to, and this is also how we tend to judge right from wrong. As a result, we are quick to stereotype things that conform to our yardstick as good, and those that don't as bad. Unfortunately, this is not the way to really see things. We are not really seeing with our own eyes but merely pigeonholing our experiences as a result of external factors, such as knowledge acquired through books or information learned from our parents. We are absorbed in our old ways of thinking; we resist change and refuse to yield. We unwittingly trigger chain reactions in which one type of pain breeds others. While we are in pain, however, we don't think that there is more pain ahead; we simply cling to the current state of affairs and reject the possibility of change as entirely out of the question.

Please try to appreciate the fact that our physical bodies have been growing and changing since birth. Change is as good as it is natural. If you are aware of this fact you can use it to your advantage; you can shift your karma in a good direction and alter your fate. Furthermore, you can link to the eternal existence and encounter it. This is the path toward true happiness.

Tap into the changes

The mind is perpetually changing. What you decided in the morning—"Yes, I am going to do this today"—may well not have happened by the evening. Our intentions can shift at a dizzying speed. At your wedding, you solemnly swore, "I will love you forever," but the feeling didn't last forever, as you promised. The mind desires change; it seeks different encounters and stimuli as soon as it becomes accustomed to a particular routine.

I mentioned earlier that we have a tendency to resist change. Staying in the same place promotes a feeling of ease, whereas change makes us anxious. On the other hand, exposure to the same stimuli over and over again can make us bored; peacefulness, too, can become wearying. When we feel like this, we go in search of different stimuli. Of course, there are times and occasions when we are able to view change as positive, such as when we go in active pursuit of exciting events. We might want to visit a different country, or to own a home, or to have an encounter with a new person. We feel invigorated and alive as new energy surges. Excessive peacefulness, in other words, can be monotonous.

The senses are always excited and activated by new stimuli. The mind, too, rejoices; it affixes to the new stimulus and expects another one to arrive as soon as the novelty has worn off. However, as you congratulate yourself for being amid such engrossing changes, you risk becoming further estranged from the path toward the truth. When you suffer one setback after another and start to feel as though you are in a negative spiral, you will grow weary of change for its own sake, and start to crave peace of mind.

At present, many of us are connected at the level of our minds and senses alone. Because of this, no matter how much we think we love and care about certain things and people, we begin to weary of them after a time, and look for new changes again. Many of us only believe in what we can verify through the five senses, which, as we have discussed, condemns us to never penetrating beneath the surface. Because of this, we never really know the truth as we continue to run about in confusion, forever oscillating between joy and pain.

If you are still reading this book, I am certain you have the ability to examine things that are more profound. Please reflect seriously on the fact that changes take place, and that these changes are linked with things we cannot see, which don't change. I am not asking you to refrain from rejoicing when the time for delight is at hand; however, I do ask you to bear in mind that joy tends not to last forever, and that change is a given. In order to transcend the fluctuations of circumstance, it is necessary to practice how to part from surface attachments. Acceptance is key; accept, as unflinchingly as you can, that all is bound to change. Once you are able to firmly accept this, it will act as a catalyst and enable you to let go. It is also a cue to awaken the conscious mind. I earnestly hope that you will seize this chance as it is presented to you.

Accept and love the not-so-holy you

Many people in the world seek material prosperity and increased convenience—that is, they pursue forms of happiness that are readily visible. Of course, it goes without saying that we all enjoy modern conveniences, but, if we go in pursuit of them too much, we run the risk of being controlled by them, which causes us to lose sight of what the essential things are in life. I am not suggesting that you deny yourself the amenities of modern life; I ask only that you realize their transient nature and take the time to look into your soul.

To do this, you must encounter what is unchangeable and unshakable within you: existence at the creative source and your true self; the being that supplies energy to all the changes that exist beyond. Once you merge with this energy, you will be reborn as a person who can control yourself, as a person who knows everything. Your consciousness will be enhanced by this experience, enabling you to live in comfort and serenity, even in an environment that is far from calm.

For this to happen, you must train correctly and maintain an even keel. As you train, your senses and thoughts will sharpen. If, however, you train on your own without the correct guidance, your mind will vacillate as you continue to distinguish between right and wrong based on your ego and the actions of those around you. It is vital to train under balanced conditions and to develop your awareness and understanding under the guidance of a Siddha master. Accept and forgive yourself, then accept and forgive those around you; then you will accept everything.

It is quite difficult, for example, to forgive another person if you have been hurt by them and you continue to hold a grudge. Nonetheless, that person's karma is merely following its own laws, and to genuinely forgive them is an opportunity for significant self-growth. Think about it. You cannot change the other person. No matter how much you agonize over the situation, it is only you who experiences pain. It is crucial to expand your consciousness by treating those around you with compassion. In doing so, the other person's mind will eventually start to change.

The world is there for you to learn about yourself. By meditating, you can purify your energies and eventually transform into a person with an open mind and an open heart. By trusting your master, by trusting in creative existence at the source, your tenderness and love will begin to emerge. Furthermore, you can cultivate your confidence as you encounter the high-order energies deep within. You cannot step forward unless you accept the present. And you must do the same with yourself: you must start liking yourself as you are, right at this moment, rather than postpone liking yourself until you are complete or improved. You must accept yourself as you are now. And, by staying centered within yourself, you will melt what is deplorable with your love. It is imperative that you accept yourself when you are far from perfect, rather than love yourself only when you are good. Accept yourself as you are, and appreciate yourself, starting in the here and now.

From here, you can begin the journey toward progress and growth. Through training, you will awaken your inner self and swiftly purify. You can cleanse your own body and mind through meditation, and the workshops of the Anugraha Himayalan Samadhi Program will enable you to transform as you progress on your journey toward perpetual existence and the divine. Remember, the eternal you is part of the divinity.

Five-minute-a-day Himalayan meditation

To generate a meditative state, purify various layers of your mind and body through thoughts, words, and actions. Support what is deep within yourself. Show appreciation. Be thankful for everything around you. Be grateful and be true to yourself.

MEDITATION USING BREATHING

Let me introduce a meditation technique that uses breathing. Breathing works to purify the mind and body. It supplies oxygen, increases metabolism, and dissolves and lessens toxins in the body. It is, in other words, a way to purify.

In breathing, there is prana, or life energy, which enhances vitality. When your mind is angered, your breath gets erratic; you can, therefore, set the mind at ease by breathing rhythmically and slowly. In other words, breathing is closely tied to the nervous system, and allows you to regulate it. Quiet, regular breathing can become a form of meditation on its own.

HIMALAYAN MEDITATION TO CALM THE FRANTIC MIND BY QUIETLY AND DEEPLY BREATHING

Envision the negative mind to be "the gray soul," and breathe it out through the mouth from the abdomen by placing both hands on the abdomen.

Completely breathe out as if squeezing the negative soul out of your body.

You will feel refreshed as you repeat the steps five times.

Even if distracting thoughts enter your mind, you can flush them away without getting caught in them. You should be able to feel that your mind and body are being cleansed.

Prepare to further deepen meditation

Assume a posture that promotes easy breathing, and, by releasing tension from the shoulders, deepen your meditation and move further in the direction of mindlessness. When distracting thoughts enter your head, concentrate on releasing them one after the other, rather than dwelling on them. Gradually empty the contents of your head.

I. THE SUKHASANA POSE TO CALM THE MIND

This is the basic seated posture to assume when meditating. You feel relaxed by easing any strain on the body, and your posture improves. By being seated, both body and mind stay in the present moment. This pose may appear ordinary, but it is an excellent way to begin to merge the body and mind as one. The ancient Himalayan Siddha masters discovered meditation as a training method to evolve humans in the direction of enlightenment; they came up with the seated pose to induce calmness in the body and mind for precisely this purpose.

In this pose, you straighten your spine vertically and cross both legs, so they create a kind of fan or anchor, enabling the posture to be comfortably sustained for very long periods.

> *Sit by extending the legs; bend the left knee inward, bringing the heel close to the crotch as the sole of the foot is held upward.*
>
> *Next, bend the right knee similarly and sit with both heels aligned.*
>
> *Pull the chin in, straighten the spine, and relax the shoulders.*
>
> *This meditative position is the completed form of the Sukhasana pose.*

2. ROTATE THE NECK TO GET RID OF EVIL THOUGHTS

Once seated in the Sukhasana pose, shed evil thoughts and assume mental concentration by cleansing energies.

> *Place both hands on the knees by turning the palms downward, and gently close the eyes.*
>
> *Straighten the spine as if your head is being pulled upward.*
>
> *Slowly rotate the head three times to the right and three times to the left, using the spine as an anchor.*

MEDITATION TO FACE YOURSELF DEEP WITHIN THE MIND

The Himalayan secret teachings define breathing as "between conscious mind and soul." By assuming the Sukhasana pose, you can purify the mind by stimulating the throat and lungs through deep breathing.

Seated in the Sukhasana pose, inhale deeply through the nose, and pay attention to the sound as you exhale by vibrating the throat as you emit the sound, "Whooo ... "

After you repeat this twenty times, you should be calm, and able to assume the state of mindlessness.

After five minutes, stretch your arms and return to the original state.

MAHAYOGA'S BREATHING MEDITATION

Breathing is a phenomenon that exists in between the conscious and unconscious minds. By focusing your attention on breathing, you will be able to maintain inner balance by becoming aware of the inner being which is not visible to you.

The following breathing exercise harnesses life energy and purifies stress. It is a meditation toward enlightenment and relaxation.

Sit in a comfortable position.

Place the palms of both hands on the knees by facing them downward.

Close your eyes.

Straighten the spine and relax the shoulders.

Next, breathe naturally.

Focus your attention on the intake of air and look at its flow.

You will be led to a wonderful, soothing world filled with relaxation.

After five minutes, stretch your arms and open your eyes.

Practice meditation in a relaxed, comfortable pose and a joyful, relaxed mood. Try not to force or push yourself too much. Choose a place that is quiet and airy and sit on a carpet or blanket to avoid feeling stiff. Wear comfortable clothes and remove your watch and any jewelry.

IMAGE MEDITATION

Image meditation develops and invigorates the right brain and helps to set the mind at ease.

Sit in a comfortable position.

Place the palms of both hands on the knees, facing downward.

Close your eyes, straighten the spine, and relax the shoulders.

Quietly contemplate your breathing for a while.

Look at the air coming out of your nose (three minutes).

Next, envision a screen in front of your eyes while the eyes are closed.

Look at the screen by focusing on a visual line slightly above the horizon.

Envision nature scenes or memorable locations visited in the past on the screen.

Then, visualize the murmur of a brook and the scent of flowers, in some detail.

By visualizing specifically, the image gets reinforced and emotions surge.

After five minutes, stretch your arms and open your eyes.

The fundamentals of the secret Himalayan teachings are communicated directly by masters. I have chosen, here, to introduce them so that I can disseminate their blessings by reaching as many people as possible. I do suggest, however, that you receive guidance directly, in order to best advance your conscious mind by deepening your meditation practice, with the aim of attaining true happiness and enlightenment.

Concluding Remarks

Become one with the universe

Samadhi is defined as becoming one with the universe by transcending time and space. I practice samadhis all the time, in privacy as well as the public samadhis in India. I consider it my mission to convey the truth to people—the truth as I have come to know it, inside and out. This is the mission entrusted to me by my guru, Hari Baba, and the Gods.

In samadhi, I become like a fire at times, sometimes like a flowing river, and sometimes I become the earth itself. I have no mind because I transcend it until I know all; I am vibration itself in its spiritual form. And I come to know everything, inside and out. I transcend my own ego, surpass its individuality, and fuse with the universe.

I exist to empower the souls of all the people I have the fortune of coming into contact with. I am not an individual. I only exist in order to raise all of your souls. What I have acquired is meant for you all. I believe it is possible that the people I have the good fortune to meet may also experience samadhi in their souls. Even if you don't perform samadhi, however, your souls will be purified by their proximity to me, and happiness will naturally come your way. You will come to know infinite truth through me. All you need to do is believe. By relaxing with me, laughing with me, meditating and praying with me, you will know boundless ability, creativity, and joy.

If you are currently experiencing tough times, please don't worry. I am praying for you. I pray so that your soul will be purified, and you will know happiness. My spiritual wishes and samadhi-level prayers are bound to directly reach your soul.

Please offer prayers now

We cannot be born of our own volition, nor can we regen-
erate when the body is ravaged by illness. We are, however,
made to survive through the wisdom of all beings. This is
the law of nature and truth. Let us learn about it together.

Peace can be realized if your inner self is filled with
love. Love and peace are indeed the very energies that turn
everything in a positive direction; they are the energies
that can allow you to be together with the divinity at all
times. I pray that you are able to feel this, even a little, and
that you can strengthen this energy as you continue to live
your life. Great love and wisdom exist within you, as does
the pure existence. Melt the clouds of your mind through
the love of your master and live powerfully by receiving
the great love and wisdom from the infinite existence that
resides deep within.

*I wish your mind will not meander in the direction of
doubt.*

I wish you to forge ahead through trust.

*You will further be blessed with graces by connecting to
meditation.*

*I wish you to return to the origin by securely harnessing
the divinity.*

*I wish you to use your mind in a positive way after
meditating in the morning, by offering gratitude for
being safe and secure for the day.*

*I wish you to continue to live by always showing gratitude,
as you stay rooted in the present moment through daily
prayers.*

I wish you to not hasten the process, but to persistently build it up.

I wish you to be able to live an enriched life by getting rid of daily troubles.

I wish you to be able to advance your conscious mind by using it as a tool to reach an enlightened state.

Please pray for world peace and for the happiness of those around you by using the mind creatively rather than negatively.

I wish you to be released from pain by linking with the sacred existence.

I wish to lend a hand so that the people around you can become happy.

I wish for more people to connect with the existence at the source of creation, link with the divinity, make meditation a habit, receive blessings, and live with peace of mind.

Please connect with my samadhi power without being restricted by my physical being; I am the existence that links with the sun within, where samadhi has been attained.

I will be your bridge to the divinity, and I will guide you. I wish for the mercies of God to shower down upon you from this bridge.

Please cultivate an unshakable trusting mind toward God.

Please ponder the act of making yourself grow, to know who you truly are by relying on your awareness through meditation.

I continue to pray for all of you

Those who can trust by giving more than a passing thought to the great, limitless, boundless existence surpassing the individual are blessed, but there are still those who choose not to believe in it. Let us understand that they have yet to forge ahead safely through trust, by stepping onto the arduous path of having to realize on their own.

I am extremely happy to have been granted this opportunity to be in touch with you. Please deepen your love by diligently continuing to meditate; please do all you can to encounter your true self.

I always wish you to be happy. I will purify your body and mind and invite you to the sacred land. There, you can encounter your true self by connecting to the existence at the sacred origin.

About the Author

Yogmata Keiko Aikawa was born in 1945 in Yamanashi Prefecture, west of Tokyo. She developed an early interest in yoga and naturopathy, which led her to travels in Tibet, China and India. She was one of earliest promoters of yoga in Japan, and in 1972 she founded the Aikawa General Health Institute, where she taught her unique Yoga Dance and Pranadi Yoga.

In 1984, she met the Siddha Master Pilot Baba while he was in Japan to perform a public Samadhi. He invited her to study among the Siddha Masters in the high Himalayas. There she met Hari Baba, who guided her through the final stages of Samadhi.

In 1991, Yogmata performed her first of many public Samadhis, a supreme yogic practice in which one is sealed in an air-tight box without food or water for seventy-two to ninety-six hours. After her eighteenth public Samadhi, she received the title of Mahamandaleshwar, or Supreme Master of the Universe, from Juna Akhara, the largest spiritual training association in India. Yogmata is the first woman and non-Indian to achieve this status.

She and Pilot Baba have held public teachings and initiations throughout the world as part of the World Peace Campaign. She is currently working with the United Nations on a series of international conferences to further universal peace, sustainable living and the leadership of women. Yogmata's charitable work includes the Yogmata Foundation, which is dedicated to funding mobile hospitals to remote villages in India. Her global mission is to bring love and kindness to all.

Today Yogmata lives in Japan. She has published over forty books.

Connect with Himalayan Wisdom

Email: usa@science.ne.jp

Twitter: @himalaya_siddha

Website: www.yogmata.com

Facebook: "yogmata"